Cambridge Elements

Elements in Soviet and Post-Soviet History
edited by
Mark Edele
University of Melbourne
Rebecca Friedman
Florida International University

UKRAINE NOT 'THE' UKRAINE

Marta Dyczok
Western University

Shaftesbury Road, Cambridge CB2 8EA, United Kingdom

One Liberty Plaza, 20th Floor, New York, NY 10006, USA

477 Williamstown Road, Port Melbourne, VIC 3207, Australia

314–321, 3rd Floor, Plot 3, Splendor Forum, Jasola District Centre, New Delhi – 110025, India

103 Penang Road, #05–06/07, Visioncrest Commercial, Singapore 238467

Cambridge University Press is part of Cambridge University Press & Assessment, a department of the University of Cambridge.

We share the University's mission to contribute to society through the pursuit of education, learning and research at the highest international levels of excellence.

www.cambridge.org
Information on this title: www.cambridge.org/9781009365574
DOI: 10.1017/9781009365536

© Marta Dyczok 2024

This work is in copyright. It is subject to statutory exceptions and to the provisions of relevant licensing agreements; with the exception of the Creative Commons version the link for which is provided below, no reproduction of any part of this work may take place without the written permission of Cambridge University Press.

An online version of this work is published at doi.org/10.1017/9781009365536 under a Creative Commons Open Access license CC-BY-NC-ND 4.0 which permits re-use, distribution and reproduction in any medium for non-commercial purposes providing appropriate credit to the original work is given. You may not distribute derivative works without permission. To view a copy of this licence, visit https://creativecommons.org/licenses/by-nc-nd/4.0/

All versions of this work may contain content reproduced under license from third parties. Permission to reproduce this third-party content must be obtained from these third-parties directly.

When citing this work, please include a reference to the DOI 10.1017/9781009365536

First published 2024

A catalogue record for this publication is available from the British Library.

ISBN 978-1-009-48604-0 Hardback
ISBN 978-1-009-36557-4 Paperback
ISSN 2753-5290 (online)
ISSN 2753-5282 (print)

Cambridge University Press & Assessment has no responsibility for the persistence or accuracy of URLs for external or third-party internet websites referred to in this publication and does not guarantee that any content on such websites is, or will remain, accurate or appropriate.

Ukraine not 'the' Ukraine

Elements in Soviet and Post-Soviet History

DOI: 10.1017/9781009365536
First published online: November 2024

Marta Dyczok
Western University

Author for correspondence: Marta Dyczok, mdyczok@uwo.ca

Abstract: This Element is a historical tour of Ukraine from the medieval Kyivan prince Volodymyr the Great through to Ukraine's twenty-first-century rock star president Volodymyr Zelensky. It presents Ukraine as an actor, not a pawn, in international history. And it focuses on people. In the past, historians wrote about Ukraine from a colonial perspective that portrayed it as a region, not its own entity. This shaped the way people thought about Ukraine and created mental maps where it was just part of something else. Put in contemporary terms, Ukraine was subjected to a historical disinformation war. This Element joins voices that are decolonizing that way of thinking by drawing a different mental map, one where Ukraine exists as itself. It explains how the people living on its lands have their own distinct history, how they shaped it, were shaped by it, and had an impact on both European and global history. This title is also available as open access on Cambridge Core.

Keywords: Ukraine, Europe, disinformation, decolonizing, Russia

© Marta Dyczok 2024

ISBNs: 9781009486040 (HB), 9781009365574 (PB), 9781009365536 (OC)
ISSNs: 2753-5290 (online), 2753-5282 (print)

Contents

Introduction — 1

1 The Princes — 3

2 The Cossacks — 11

3 The Nation Builders — 20

4 The State Builders — 34

5 The Defenders — 44

Conclusion — 58

Further Reading — 60

References — 64

Introduction

On 22 June 2022, Max, my former PhD student, was somewhere on the front line in Ukraine. He posted a photo of himself video-chatting with his two-year-old son on Facebook, which he titled 'Screenshot by Volodymyr Sviezhentsev'(Sviezhentsev, 2022b). They were both smiling. A week earlier he had written, 'The hardest thing so far is not the routine, not the patrolling, not even the shelling although that is frightening, but not being able to see my little boy' (Sviezhentsev, 2022a). When Russia escalated its war against Ukraine, Max volunteered to defend his country. Russia's president Vladimir Putin claimed that Ukraine did not exist as a nation. But Max, and tens of thousands like him who were willing to risk their lives to protect Ukraine, showed the world that it did.

Max was born in Crimea to a Ukrainian mother and Russian military officer father in 1991, the year that Ukraine gained modern independence. He grew up speaking Russian, later came to Canada where he completed a PhD in history at Western University, and then went back to Ukraine. When Russia threatened a full-scale invasion, Max left his job in Kyiv, put his promising academic career on hold, kissed his wife and toddler son goodbye, and signed up for the country's Territorial Defence. A few days later, the attack came. Max was with his unit. His wife took their little boy, left the capital Kyiv, and headed west. Communication between them was intermittent. Then on 18 June, Max's unit was connected to Starlink and they were able to video-chat. His little boy had learned to do screenshots! Thanks to the internet and modern technology, Max could talk to his son, and Ukraine was able to show the world how it was opposing the Russian attack.

Many of Max's former professors and fellow students in Canada were following his story. He was posting on social media and was regularly interviewed by the international press. Back when he had been working on his doctorate at Western University, Max often had to explain that he was from Ukraine, not 'the' Ukraine, which is how many still referred to his country (Graber, 2022). Most people he met had learned about Ukraine through the prism of Russian imperial history. In that version, Ukraine is presented as part of other histories – a region, the south, 'Little Russia' – not as a place with its own history. In some ways, this is not too different from how many histories of Great Britain look upon Ireland, Scotland, and Wales. Or how Indigenous peoples used to be written about in Canada, the USA, Australia, and other former colonies. Those in power usually write history to suit their interests, for example writing that Europeans 'discovered' North America and 'civilized' the people living there, rather than describing the reality that they had colonized the continent.

Russian president Putin regularly claimed that Ukraine is not a nation and that it had always been part of Russia. Numerous international observers shared this colonial view, or a version of it, suggesting that Russia had a right to exercise influence over Ukraine for historical or geopolitical reasons. This is in part because of the way they learned history. If someone has been taught that Ukraine is and has always been an integral part of Russia, this shapes the mental maps they carry around in their heads. For most of its history, Ukraine was in fact part of Europe, and western Ukraine remained so until 1944. But because Ukraine did not have its own modern state until 1991, those who controlled its territory had the power to write its history. Ukrainian historians were often not heard. One could say that Ukraine has been on the receiving end of a historical disinformation war for centuries.

This Element is about Ukraine as a nation with its own history, not 'the' Ukraine. It dispels and decolonizes old ways of thinking and draws a different map – one where the people living on the lands currently within its borders shaped their own history, were shaped by it, and influenced European and global history. Think of it as a whirlwind historical tour: from the times of the medieval Kyivan grand prince Volodymyr the Great to Ukraine's twenty-first-century rock-star president Volodymyr Zelensky. The story begins with the civilization of Kyivan Rus, where princes ruled the land and shaped the history of the region. Centuries later, the name Rus would be appropriated by Muscovite Tsar Ivan IV, also known as Ivan the Terrible. The story continues with the Cossacks who created an early form of democracy in central Ukraine and shifted the power balance in Eastern Europe. Then comes the late modern era when people in Europe started to think of themselves as nations. Poets, historians, and politicians in Ukraine did the same. The last two sections look at Ukraine after it became a modern European state in 1991. It finally reappeared on the world map and embarked on the task of state-building, only to have Russia invade again in 2014. This began a new era of Ukraine defending itself against a much larger state.

The lives of people living in what is today Ukraine have always been closely intertwined with their neighbours to their west, east, north, and south. The reader will see how throughout this complex history, power and borders shifted, elites and ordinary people made choices, and identity was fluid and contested. There is a focus on human agency, what scholars describe as an individual's capacity to act in a given environment (Mayr, 2011). This will help explain why Ukraine did not surrender to Russia, as many expected it to. When Russia marched on Kyiv on 24 February 2022, President Zelensky said: 'We are not putting down arms. We will be defending our country, because our weapon is truth, and our truth is that this is our land, our country, our children, and we will defend all of this' (Zelensky on Twitter, 26 February 2022). Zelensky was echoing what the people of Ukraine have been saying and doing for centuries.

Interestingly, in 2022 the presidents of Ukraine and Russia shared a first name, Volodymyr/Vladimir. It is the name of the ancient Grand Prince of Kyiv. And the name Max chose for his son.

1 The Princes

Introduction

Kyiv was once the centre of a large and powerful European civilization. Historians call it Kyivan Rus, and it existed in the late Middle Ages, from the ninth to the thirteenth century. Princes ruled the land, and many of Kyiv's famous golden-domed churches date back to this period. Ukrainians trace their beginnings to this time when they write about their 1,000 years of history. Kyivan Rus was not a modern state but rather a loose federation of city-states and principalities ruled by various princes, with Kyiv as the capital. Many foundations for society were laid during this era: Orthodox Christianity was adopted, literacy was introduced, laws were codified, money was minted, borders were fortified, and relations with the rest of Europe were established. At its high point, Kyivan Rus spanned a territory covering about a third of Europe, from the Carpathian Mountains in the west to the Volga River in the east, from the Black Sea in the south to the Baltic Sea in the north (Higasi, 2017; Magocsi, 1987).

During this golden era, a Kyivan princess was sent off to marry the king of France. Princess Anne of Kyiv could read and write in several languages. She arrived in Paris only to discover that her husband, Henri I, was illiterate and that her new home was less opulent and far less clean than what she was accustomed to. After he died, Anne ruled France as co-regent until their son Philip I came of age, a remarkable accomplishment for a European woman at that time. Her signature on a royal charter has been on public display in France to this very day (Zajac, 2018).

The princes of Rus built a kingdom while fighting off intruders, and each other, for control of the capital. Eventually, the invasions, infighting, and changing trade patterns weakened the confederation. The final blow came from the east in 1240 when the Mongols attacked and destroyed Kyiv as a centre of power. Rus, as it had been, ceased to exist. Other political powers gained control over different parts of the Rus lands, and they developed into distinct states that would eventually become Ukraine, Belarus, and Russia.

This era is key to understanding present-day relations between Ukraine and Russia because of the different ways in which historians later wrote about it. There are few records from this time, and much of what we know about Kyivan Rus is based on legends, myths, and documents written centuries after the events they describe. What we do know is that Kyiv, the capital of modern Ukraine, was the centre of the Rus civilization. Ukrainian historians trace their history back to this era. At that time, Moscow was a small town almost 500 miles to the north, with no political significance. It would gradually take over parts of the old Rus and become a large empire, even adopting the name Rus, which with time evolved into Russia. The country's historians would later construct an origin story that claimed a monopoly on the legacy of Kyivan Rus, arguing that Kyiv was the cradle of their civilization and that Ukrainians and Russians have been one people since the times of Kyivan Rus. This Russian colonial version of history was exported to the world and has shaped mental maps well into the present. In 2021, shortly before launching his all-out war against Ukraine, Russian president Putin published a summary of this view in an essay titled 'On the Historical Unity of Russians and Ukrainians' (Putin, 2021).

Back in the Middle Ages, people didn't think of themselves in terms of nations. Princes, kings, warlords, emperors, Vikings, and knights competed for power, resources, land, and trade routes. It was a violent time when civilizations rose and fell, slave trading was the norm, and religion exerted tremendous control.

The Vikings

Kyivan Rus appeared in the late ninth century, but people lived on the lands that are today Ukraine as far back as the Stone Age. For centuries, various populations journeyed through these territories, as they did all over Europe and Asia. Some settled, while others moved on. Archaeologists discovered elaborately decorated artefacts with swirling patterns left behind by the Trypillians, tribes that lived south of Kyiv over 6,000 years ago. The ancient Greeks set up colonies along the Black Sea around the sixth and seventh centuries BC and traded with the people living to their north. Ruins and columns from that era can still be found in Ukraine today, as well as place names they gave to settlements such as Feodosia (in Crimea) and Kherson. The famous Greek historian Herodotus wrote about travels up the Dnipro River, which runs north–south down the centre of Ukraine. He described the people who lived there, the Scythians. They had come from Asia a century or so before the Greeks, conquered much of today's Ukraine, stayed for some 400 years, and left behind exquisite gold artefacts that are now on display in museums both in Ukraine and abroad. Sometime at the beginning of the first millennium AD, Slavs migrated from central Europe, settled in the east, and began farming and hunting. The early Slavs were made up of different tribes and are considered the early ancestors of Ukrainians, Belarusians, and Russians. Sometimes they cooperated and other times fought among each other, often encountering other migrating peoples, some of whom were peaceful and many of whom were not.

So, what led to the emergence of Kyivan Rus? According to most historians, it had its roots in the Viking Age. Before Kyivan Rus took shape, there was a kingdom to the east of the Slavs known as the Khazar Khaganate whose elite had converted to Judaism. They were forcing the Slavs to pay tribute (*danyna*) to them, a form of tax, including in slaves, which the Slavs resented and periodically rebelled against. In the west, there were several small kingdoms such as Bulgaria and Moravia, with which they had some contact. To their south, lying on the other side of the Black Sea, the powerful and wealthy Byzantine Empire ruled.

Around 793, Scandinavians began exploring the world looking for trade, conquest, and, according to some sources, women. While some of these fierce warrior-traders used their famous longboats to reach western Europe and cross the Atlantic, others rowed east and south (Duczko, 2004). They had heard of the riches of Byzantium and the famous colourful markets of the Arab world and were looking for river routes to find them. Firstly, they headed down the Volga River in today's Russia but were blocked by the Khazars. They then made their way along the Dnipro River in Ukraine. Along the way, they discovered numerous settlements. One of them was Kyiv.

There are many legends and myths surrounding the founding of Kyiv. An early one says that the apostle Andrew once stood on the hills on the right bank of the Dnipro River and proclaimed: 'Someday a great city will be built here.' Another says that the Viking brothers Askold and Dir founded the city; there is a spot called Askold's Grave in a park in central Kyiv today. Perhaps the most popular legend revolves around three other Viking brothers called Kyi, Shchek, and Khoryv, and their sister Lybid. The story is that they were travelling down the Dnipro in search of Byzantium when they came upon a pretty town and decided to settle there. The city is said to have been named after Kyi, hence Kyiv. A large statue of these explorer-founders now stands on the banks of the Dnipro River near the city centre and is a popular tourist spot. Many Viking warriors were doing the same during those turbulent times. They navigated along rivers, came across settlements such as Chernihiv and Pereiaslav (now both in Ukraine), Polatsk (now in Belarus), and Smolensk (now in Russia), conquered them and set up their own principalities.

According to an ancient document written by medieval Kyiv monks called the Primary Chronicle, a Viking leader called Helgi/Oleh/Oleg became the Prince of Kyiv in 882. He is considered the founder of Kyivan Rus. Helgi was his Scandinavian name, but since the people he came to rule were Slavs his name was adapted to their language and he became Oleh (Ukrainian) or Oleg (Russian). By the time he was said to have come to rule Kyiv, it was already an established city since it was in a prime location, at the intersection of important trade routes. Helgi/Oleh/Oleg, who is believed to have come from the more northern city of Novgorod, united the various Slavic tribes, fended off the Khazars from the east, and established trade relations with Byzantium in the south. Legend has it that he tried to defy a prophecy that his stallion would cause his death by sending the horse away, only to be bitten by a deadly serpent that crawled out of its skull following the animal's death.

The name Rus came with these Vikings who gradually began to rule the land. Like so much from this era the exact origin of the word is disputed. Some say it originates from the old Finnish word *Ruotsi*, which means 'the men who row' and was used to describe the Swedes. Others say it stems from Roslagen, a Swedish coastal area. Whatever its origin, Rus became the name of the emerging polity and its people, and we know this because that is how the Byzantines referred to them in their written records.

For the first century or so, Rus princes ruled their individual realms, but over time they began cooperating and soon formed a loose federation. Often they would unite to defend themselves from recurring incursions by invaders. Other times, they competed among themselves for the Kyiv throne – the title of Grand Prince of Kyiv and the power that went with it. These quests for control were often bloody. But trade from the Baltic to the Black Sea increased, including in slaves; the economy grew and with it the population increased; many new towns began appearing; and Kyivan Rus began its golden era.

The Great and Wise Grand Princes

The most famous Kyivan grand princes are Volodymyr and Yaroslav, who ruled roughly from 980 to 1054. Historians have called them Volodymyr the Great and Yaroslav the Wise, and their images appear on the currency of modern Ukraine. Volodymyr/Vladimir, whose Scandinavian name was Valdamar, captured the Kyiv throne through a series of wars with his brothers. Once he gained power in 980, he took the kingdom to greatness. His armies expanded the territories of Kyivan Rus to the largest they would be, a third of the size of Europe. He then secured the perimeter by building a series of forts to protect the territories and people in his realm.

Volodymyr/Vladimir also took a decision that changed Rus history – he introduced Christianity to the land. His grandmother, the legendary Princess Olha/Olga/Helga, had already laid the groundwork for this, having adopted Christianity as her personal religion years earlier. The Slavs and Vikings, however, were pagans, and Volodymyr had at least five wives and supposedly 100 concubines. But in 988 he too converted to Christianity, reportedly married the Byzantine Emperor's sister, took her brother's name Basil (which he never used), and brought Christianity to Kyivan Rus. How this came about is also steeped in legend. Some say that Volodymyr sent emissaries out into the world to learn about all the major religions. When the envoys from Byzantium returned, they described visiting the Hagia Sophia Cathedral in Constantinople, which was the capital of Byzantium, now modern-day Istanbul. The beauty of the frescos and the singing of the choir made them feel as though they were in heaven, and they convinced Volodymyr that this was the religion to adopt. A cathedral also called Sophia was later built in Kyiv. In reality, Volodymyr's decision to embrace Christianity was a pragmatic one. The Byzantine Empire was the major power in the region, and adopting its religion was an astute political move.

Volodymyr understood that religion was a vehicle into the Christian world, and with it came an entire civilization 'package': status, literacy, culture, improved security, and foreign and trade relations. New elites would emerge who could read, write, and develop the principality, and they would no longer be considered barbarians. However, because Rus adopted Christianity from Byzantium, it would become part of the Eastern Orthodox world after the Great Schism, when Christians split into two separate religions, Catholic and Orthodox. This would affect the region's relations with its neighbours for centuries to come.

Volodymyr introduced many advancements to Kyivan Rus. He allocated a tenth of his wealth to developing Christianity. The money was spent building churches and monasteries, as well as schools and libraries since that is where learning was based. Priests, monks, and bishops were invited from Byzantium, as well as architects, craftsmen, and new tradesmen. Volodymyr also set up a new system of governance, the Great Council of Boyars. *Boyar* is the Rus word for nobles. He invited members of his Viking entourage and local Slavic leaders to sit on the Council and gave them the power to make political decisions. A currency was created with minted silver coins that had a trident imprinted on them, and this same trident would later be adopted as the symbol of modern Ukraine. To bring harmony to the various principalities of Kyivan Rus, Volodymyr divided the realm into twelve kingdoms and placed a legitimate son on each of the thrones. The oldest one was to succeed him as the Grand Prince of Kyiv. Regrettably, but perhaps not surprisingly, this transfer of power did not work, and following his death, Volodymyr's sons fought among themselves for the Kyiv throne for the next decade.

Yaroslav eventually won and he took Kyivan Rus to new heights. He transformed Kyiv into one of the most beautiful cities in Europe, and many of the landmarks built in his time are still standing. His massive construction project expanded Kyiv's upper city where the elites lived, and it was fortified with ramparts, gates, and palisades. The main entrance to the city became the Golden Gate, like in Constantinople, which centuries later would become the subject of Modest Mussorgsky's musical work 'The Great Gate of Kyiv'. Yaroslav also commissioned the construction of grand religious and secular buildings, the most famous one being the St Sophia Cathedral, named after the cathedral in Constantinople. It has withstood centuries of invaders and assaults, even Nazi shelling, and stands to this very day.

To increase the independence of his realm in the religious sphere, Yaroslav established a separate Metropolitan of Rus, thus removing Kyivan Rus from the direct control of the Orthodox Church in Byzantium. Church Slavonic was introduced as the official church language instead of the Greek that Byzantium was using, and the Cyrillic alphabet was adopted. Reportedly an avid reader, Yaroslav promoted intellectual life and began the process of recording history – he commissioned monks to write chronicles, as was the custom in Byzantium. This was when work on the Primary Chronicle began, and from this period onward there are written records that give us a clearer picture of events.

Laws were also written down on Yaroslav's orders in a document called 'Ruska Pravda', which became one of the first written legal codes in Europe. From this we know that Yaroslav made life in his realm more humane: punishments were changed from those of a violent nature to monetary payments, there was a move away from slavery, and land rights began to be codified, including women's rights. Kyiv became an important political and economic European capital, and foreign visitors to the city often described its beauty and the opulence of its court in their writings.

To strengthen Kyivan Rus internationally, Yaroslav actively engaged in marriage diplomacy and became known as the father-in-law of Europe. He himself married a Swedish princess and arranged marriages for his children with kingdoms where he sought to build alliances. His favourite daughter Anne, mentioned earlier, was sent to France, and her sisters were married off to the kings of Norway and Hungary. Yaroslav's sons wed the royal daughters of Poland, Byzantium, and Saxony, and a granddaughter of Henry II, the Holy Roman Emperor.

Throughout this period, the economy grew, agricultural production and trade increased, and so did the population. By the twelfth century, between seven and eight million people were living in Kyivan Rus, 13 per cent of them in cities, which was unusual for that time. Kyiv had become one of the largest cities in Europe with a population of 40,000 to 50,000, a size London would reach only two centuries later. It is said that when Anne arrived in her new Paris home, she was disappointed to find the French capital smaller, darker, and somewhat less clean than what she was used to. It was also during this era that Kyivan Rus society developed into different strata. The upper classes were the ruling elite (the princes and their families), followed by the nobility and church people; the rest were townspeople, peasants, and slaves. Most people lived in the countryside, which also left them vulnerable to both invaders and the nobility that taxed them.

Princes in the other Rus kingdoms followed Kyiv's example and built their own cathedrals, schools, and libraries. Like the Grand Prince of Kyiv, they regulated the economy through taxation and allocation of lands. But they could not agree on the succession principle, and after Yaroslav's death, they fought for control of Kyiv in clashes that went on for years. Gradually, some princes became comfortable in their own capitals. They concentrated on developing their principalities and grew less interested in Kyiv. Trade patterns began to shift from north–south to east–west and this led to further diffusion and loss of unity. Kyivan Rus started to decentralize as a result. The Halych–Volhyn principality in the west remained influential and prosperous, but invaders kept coming from the east and the disunited kingdom was not able to withstand the repeated attacks. The final blow came when the Mongols attacked Kyiv.

The Mongols, the Lithuanians, and the Poles

Batu Khan led the Mongol army that destroyed Kyiv as a political capital in 1240. The Mongols were known as the Golden Horde because their tents were a golden colour and their huge armies attacked quickly on horseback. Batu was the grandson of the famous Genghis Khan who had founded the Mongol Empire, and it was Batu who expanded it into the largest contiguous (overland) empire in the world. The skilled leader was reportedly rather short and kind to his family, but a ferocious warrior. His powerful armies swept through Asia, absorbing people along the way such as the Tatars, which is why they were eventually called both Mongols and Tatars. Batu advanced into Europe, making it as far as Hungary and conquering everything along the way, including the kingdoms of Kyivan Rus.

Unlike the Viking leaders, Batu Khan did not settle in Kyiv but turned east to set up his base in what is now southern Russia, near the Volga River in an area called Sarai. He ruled his empire from there. The Mongols were much feared, and Russian historians have written about their rule as the Tatar Yoke. But in fact, Batu's goal was not destruction but rather power and wealth, and other historians have called his era the *Pax Mongolica*, Latin for 'Mongol peace'. Once Batu conquered an area, he would force it to submit to his authority and pay taxes, including in slaves, but otherwise left people to get on with their affairs. After the nearly complete destruction of Kyiv, the Rus princes were left in peace as long as they recognized Batu's authority. The Orthodox Church flourished, and nobles, townspeople, peasants, and slaves continued their lives much as they had before. Gradually, the various principalities came under different influences and their histories began to diverge.

The Mongol Empire expanded into the south-eastern area of today's Ukraine along the Azov and Black Sea coasts. This included the Crimean Peninsula, an important region in the east–west trade routes, and that is how the Tatars came to settle there. In the north, a few Rus principalities resisted the Golden Horde, but the emerging Muscovy's rulers generally cooperated with them, intermarried with their elites, and carved out a role for themselves as the Horde's tax collector in the area. This allowed them to increase their power over their neighbours, and some see this as the origin of Moscow's autocracy. Moscow gradually became the centre of a state that would turn into an empire and later call itself Russia, laying exclusive claim to the heritage of Rus. The westernmost Rus principalities of Halych–Volhyn came to an agreement with the Horde that gave them a degree of autonomy for a while, but they came under increasing pressure from their western Catholic neighbours, Hungary and Poland. Over time, the Golden Horde began experiencing internal divisions. Then came the Black Death, the bubonic plague pandemic. This weakened the Mongol kingdom further. It disintegrated into smaller khanates, with the Crimean Khanate becoming the most powerful kingdom in the south.

As the Golden Horde's influence weakened, a new power began expanding from the north-west into the old Rus principalities that are now Ukraine: the Grand Duchy of Lithuania. Teutonic Knights were pressing in on the pagan Lithuanians from the west, so they began expanding eastward into the old Rus lands. Today, Lithuania is a small country, but it was once the largest kingdom in Eastern Europe. Their monarch Gediminas assumed the Kyiv throne in the fourteenth century, took the title Grand Duke of Lithuania and Rus, and embraced the Rus heritage. This is known as the Lithuanian period of Ukrainian history. Rather than imposing their rule, the Lithuanians adopted much from the lands of Rus. They took Orthodox Christianity as their official religion, and the Rus administrative system was introduced to their entire realm, including their legal and social structures. The Rus princes and nobility were accepted into the ruling elite, and Jews continued to be welcomed in cities, growing in number during this time.

In due course, Lithuania came under renewed pressure from the Teutonic Knights in the west while experiencing growing threats from an expanding Moscow Principality in the north-east. They turned to Poland for help. What started as a marriage between a thirty-five-year-old Lithuanian king and twelve-year-old Polish queen eventually evolved into the Polish–Lithuanian Commonwealth, with Poland gradually taking the upper hand.

This changed things considerably for people living on Ukrainian lands, in part because Poland was a Catholic kingdom and introduced new patterns of colonization. Elites living in what is now Ukraine lost political power over their own affairs. But soon they would create a new phenomenon that became the stuff of legend – the Cossacks.

2 The Cossacks

Introduction

Cossacks have long aroused the world's imagination. They lived in central Ukraine from the mid fifteenth to the late eighteenth century and have been immortalized in art from the British romantic Lord Byron and Ukrainian ballads to modern-day films. Images of skilful warriors riding through the Ukrainian steppes on horseback in their distinctive hats, fighting for freedom, have become legendary. What is often missing from these colourful portrayals is the political importance of the Cossacks. Few books mention that Ukrainian Cossacks led the largest successful anti-colonial uprising in Europe of the seventeenth century. Their armies peaked at around 100,000, moved across more than 600 miles in just one summer, and successfully rebelled against one of the biggest powers in Europe at the time, the Polish–Lithuanian Commonwealth. As a result, two things happened. The Cossacks created the first modern Ukrainian state, which was a new kind of sociopolitical entity they called the Hetmanate. It had elements of democracy and led to a new kind of identity. They didn't yet think of themselves in terms of a nation but saw themselves as descendants of Rus and distinct from Poles and Muscovites. Secondly, the Cossacks shifted the balance of power in Eastern Europe. They permanently weakened Poland and, unintentionally, opened of the door for Muscovy to further expand its growing empire into Eastern Europe. (Rudnytsky, 1987).

Bohdan Khmelnytsky is a key but controversial figure from this period. There is a large statue of him in central Kyiv right next to the St Sophia Cathedral. He sits on horseback in full Cossack regalia, including a feathered hetman hat, pointing his bulava (mace) north-east towards Moscow. Hetman was the title Cossacks gave their military commanders, and the bulava signified Khmelnytsky was a hetman of the highest military rank. The bulava would later be adopted by modern Ukraine as a symbol of presidential power. Khmelnytsky was the hetman who led the successful seventeenth-century uprising that freed many Ukrainian lands from Polish rule, but in the process, numerous Poles and Jews were killed, and the Cossack leader is depicted as a villain in their historiographies. Khmelnytsky is also responsible for creating the Hetmanate; however, he later negotiated an agreement with Muscovite tsar Alexei Mikhailovich that would lead to the gradual loss of the Cossacks' newfound independence. As a result, Ukrainian historians write that Khmelnytsky left behind a mixed legacy, while Russian historians portray him as a hero who reunited the two peoples.

The Cossack phenomenon was a reaction by people living on the lands that are today central Ukraine who wanted to assert control over their own affairs amidst complex social and religious tensions and rapidly changing global developments. The word Cossack comes from the Turkic *kazak* or *qazaq*, loosely translated as 'free man, freebooting warrior and raider'. It describes people who could not, or chose not to, find their place in the societies where they lived and instead journeyed to the open steppes where they created their own way of life. The Cossack era had three distinct phases: its emergence, the creation of the Hetmanate, and its gradual incorporation into Muscovy. Cossacks shaped the history on Ukrainian lands during this era but, as in previous centuries, the actions of people who lived there both influenced and were influenced by changes around them. These included the population explosion in Western Europe, the Renaissance, changing economic and religious patterns, and the political fortunes of their neighbours.

The Rebels

The Cossack era began in the mid fifteenth century, when the lands of central Ukraine were a quasi-political no-man's land. People of various social strata lived there, both in cities and the countryside, but there was no political entity that fully controlled them. Soon, however, changes started happening around the old Rus lands.

In the south, the Tatar Khanate came to control the Crimean Peninsula and the northern Black Sea coast. It had branched off when the Golden Horde was disintegrating and established good relations with the Ottoman Turkish Empire, which had settled on the other side of the Black Sea after overrunning the Orthodox Byzantines. Much of the Tatar economy was based on the slave trade. Since Muslims were not allowed to enslave other Muslims, they hunted for slaves in the southern and central areas of what is today Ukraine. They targeted the inhabitants, who had been Christianized by the Rus princes, and sold them to the Ottomans. This made it a dangerous land zone and led to the gradual depopulation of the area – until the Cossacks appeared.

In the north-east, the Principality of Muscovy began emerging as a new regional power. It had already gained prominence as the tax collector for the Golden Horde, but as the Mongol Empire weakened, Moscow broke away and began an imperial expansion of its own. Using the military skills learned from its former Mongol masters, Muscovy first conquered Orthodox principalities in the European part of modern Russia, which had been part of Rus. It then turned south and captured the remaining lands of the Golden Horde, including Kazan, which was Muslim. Muscovy next set its sights on the Baltic territories then known as Livonia, but that attempt failed. The Scandinavians (Sweden, Norway, Denmark) came to Livonia's defence, as did Lithuania, which at that time ruled much of old Rus.

The Livonian War made it clear to Lithuania that Muscovy was becoming a real threat. The two kingdoms had fought previously over territories and the legacy of Rus. But now Lithuania understood that things were changing, and it decided to strengthen its links with Poland, its neighbour to the south-west. The two countries turned their existing dynastic union into a formal arrangement and created the Polish–Lithuanian Commonwealth through the 1569 Lublin Treaty. This had serious consequences for the lands of Ukraine. Poland and Lithuania divided the territories of old Rus and defined its borders. Lithuania took over the lands which would become Belarus, while Poland assumed control of what would become Ukraine. The name Ukraine appears at this time on the first known map of the area, created by the Pole Tomasz Makowski in the 1590s (Seegel, 2013).

Poland was a very different kind of kingdom than the people of Rus had previously encountered. It was part of the Catholic Christian world, which at the time was going through the Renaissance and Reformation. In Poland's political system, the nobility was powerful, enjoyed extensive rights, and elected their king. Unlike the Lithuanians who had adopted Rus practices, the Poles brought their own language, religion, culture, and politics to the Rus lands. Rus princes and nobility initially accepted the Polish kingdom, seeing it as protection from attacks by the Tatars and Muscovites. Some adopted Polish ways, including the language and religion. Terms such as 'a Pole of Rus Origin' and 'Polish Rus' would later appear to describe them, as well as Ruthenian, the Latinized version of Rus, suggesting that they continued to see themselves, and be seen, as the people of Rus.

Others in the Rus lands kept their old Orthodox ways and did very well. For example, Prince Konstantyn Ostrozky came to own large parts of western Ukraine, including 40 castles, 1,000 towns, and 13,000 villages. He also kept an army of 20,000 men. Ostrozky was a pretender to both the Polish and Moscow crowns, but he saw himself as continuing the work of the Rus princes Volodymyr and Yaroslav and embarked on numerous cultural initiatives. Drawing inspiration from European advancements making their way through Poland, he set up a scholarly academy, invited international academics to teach there, and set up a publishing project that produced the first printed bible in Church Slavonic in 1580. Another powerful family were the Vyshnevetskys who owned large tracts of land in central Ukraine that were vulnerable to Tatar raids. In the mid-1500s Dmytro Vyshnevetsky built a fortress on an island about halfway down the Dnipro River as an outpost against them. It would become known as the Zaporozhian Sich and according to folk tradition he would become the first Hetman of the Cossacks.

So, who were these Cossacks and where did they come from? There aren't many reliable records from their early period, but what is known is that they were both nobles and peasants rebelling against the new order Poland was creating. The Polish king was granting land in Ukraine to the Polish nobility, and they were setting up large manorial estates which some called a form of colonization or a land grab. Western Europe was experiencing a population explosion, and this was creating an expanding market for grain and other raw materials. The lands in central Ukraine are very fertile, and as Poland began taking them over in the sixteenth century, it began acquiring great wealth from the grain trade. Its exports grew twentyfold in just over 100 years. This is when Ukraine developed its reputation as the 'breadbasket of Europe'.

Part of the increase in grain production was because the new landlords began imposing growing demands on and restricting the freedoms of peasants who worked the land. It was common throughout Europe for nobles to demand that peasants work on their lands as a form of rent. But during this period the Polish nobles kept increasing the number of days of this unpaid labour. Peasants began fleeing to estates which were less restrictive or into areas which were not yet controlled by nobles: the steppes in central and southern Ukraine. There, they formed groups and lived off the land, hunting, fishing, trapping, and learning to defend themselves. They also engaged in banditry and occasional raids against the Tatars to plunder and sometimes free slaves. They became known as Cossacks. Some set up fortified centres, but once the Zaporozhian Sich fortress on the Dnipro was built, it became their main one, their nerve centre. The Cossacks living there governed themselves on the principle of equality, and decisions were taken at general meetings called Rada. The term would later be adopted by modern Ukraine for the country's political legislature. Not all Cossacks lived at the Sich; many resided in settlements with their families.

Over time, the Cossacks developed into a political and military force. Their reputation as courageous warriors led some nobles, including Prince Ostrozky, to recruit them into their service. Later, the Polish king began doing the same. Poland had only a small standing army, so it engaged Cossack units to fight in wars all over Europe. The Rus horsemen gained valuable experience and expanded their reputation as accomplished fighters. Gradually, the arrangement was formalized and those Cossacks serving Poland became known as Registered Cossacks since they were treated as soldiers of the kingdom. They were exempted from paying taxes and given salaries and rights that eventually included property rights. Over time, a new Cossack class emerged. This led to divisions among the Cossacks since only a small number were registered. Many Cossacks remained unregistered with no salaries or property rights and continued to live as they always had. The number of Registered Cossacks would rise and fall depending on the needs of the commonwealth – anywhere from 20,000 to 1,000. It was not unusual for numbers to be reduced after a successful military campaign when their services were no longer needed. This led to discontent and rebellions that Poland usually suppressed or, alternatively, accommodated by granting privileges to the Cossack elites.

The relationship between landlords, peasants, and Cossacks was not the only source of tension. Another was religion. The Polish–Lithuanian Commonwealth was experiencing the Counter-Reformation, and this led to increasing disputes over religion on Ukrainian lands, whose inhabitants were predominantly Orthodox. There was an attempt to bring Catholics and Orthodox Christians together under the jurisdiction of the pope: in 1596 an agreement called the Union of Brest was concluded, creating the Ukrainian Greek Catholic (Uniate) Church. Some Orthodox clergy agreed with this decision, while others opposed it, and this led to a religious split that continues into the present. By this time the Kyiv region had become de facto controlled by the Cossacks, and they made Kyiv the centre of Orthodox religion, culture and education. The old capital began experiencing a revival in part inspired by the Renaissance, what historian Serhii Plokhii (2014) called 'the Westernization of the Byzantine heritage'. Most importantly the Cossack elite began to position themselves as protectors of the Orthodox faith.

Adding to these strains was the situation of the region's Jewish population. They had lived on Ukrainian lands from the times of Rus but, as Poland took over, Jews began migrating there in larger numbers and their population grew to around 50,000 in the seventeenth century. They set about establishing communities, building synagogues, and opening schools, but Poland would not allow them to own land. Many of the new Polish landowners, who also owned the mills used for processing grain and held exclusive rights to alcohol production, wanted to exploit the land but not actually manage their estates. So, they introduced a system called arenda where they leased their properties to administrators and gave them the authority to manage them and collect taxes on their behalf. For the most part, these positions were given to Jews who also became the main moneylenders in the land. This put them in the middle of a tense situation. Jewish managers were collecting taxes for Catholic nobles from Orthodox peasants. A Polish saying from the time described the arrangement as 'heaven for the nobles, purgatory for the townspeople, hell for the peasants, and paradise for the Jews' (Gromelski, 2013; Konieczny, 2021).

The final component in this volatile mix were disgruntled Ukrainian/Rus landowners. Polish kings were elected, so they allocated and reallocated lands in Ukraine to various nobles to gain support and influence. At times, Polish nobles would take matters into their own hands on these lands, which were in effect a frontier. They would impose their will or even take control of land belonging to local Ukrainian/Rus nobles, who would then appeal to the king for justice or restitution. If that failed, they would often join the Cossacks at their fortress in Zaporizhzhia. This is precisely what happened with Bohdan Khmelnytsky.

The Hetmans

Bohdan Khmelnytsky probably could not have imagined the pivotal role he would play in Ukrainian history. Born in 1595 or 1596 into a minor noble family in the central Ukrainian region of Chyhyryn, Khmelnytsky was given an education and then followed in the footsteps of his father into Registered Cossack military service. He reportedly served in many military campaigns, including some in western Europe where he gained international experience and a reputation as a skilful leader. Then he ran into problems with Polish nobles who raided his estate, allegedly over a dispute involving a woman. After appealing to the Polish king for justice, and failing in this effort, Khmelnytsky gathered a small detachment of his men and headed for the Zaporozhian Sich. There, the free Cossacks elected him as their hetman, and in 1648 he led them in a small uprising that turned into a mass movement. When his troops outmanoeuvred and defeated larger Polish forces, news of his successes began to spread, and more people joined him in rebelling against the Polish–Lithuanian Commonwealth. Khmelnytsky negotiated an alliance with the Crimean Tatars, and Registered Cossack detachments sent by Poland to quash the uprising instead began to switch sides and join the Zaporozhian Cossacks. Poland sent larger armies, but the rebellion kept growing and became increasingly brutal. Polish and Cossack armies killed not only each other but many civilians, including nobles, women, children, clergy, and both Poles and Jews (Sysyn, 2003).

By autumn 1648, Khmelnytsky's armies had swelled to 100,000 men. Within months, they travelled across a huge swathe of Ukraine on horseback reaching Lviv, a city deep in western Ukraine close to the Polish border. It lies around 600 miles from where they had started in Zaporizhzhia. After laying siege to Lviv, Khmelnytsky ordered his troops to withdraw. He tried to negotiate peace with the Polish king, explaining that his goal was not destruction but restoration of justice. But these efforts proved unsuccessful and the war continued. In December, Khmelnytsky arrived in Kyiv, the old Rus capital, and was welcomed as a great liberator. According to some historians, this is where his vision changed. It went from wanting to restore people's rights to seeing himself as the liberator of the Rus people living in the Polish–Lithuanian Commonwealth. The size and strength of the rebellion must have frightened the Poles because a year after it began, they agreed to allow the Cossacks to rule over the areas of Kyiv, Bratyslav, and Chernihiv in the heartland of Ukraine.

And so, in 1649 the Cossacks set up their own state. They called it the Hetmanate, with the hetman as their head of state. Khmelnytsky chose his ancestral estate, Chyhyryn, as its capital and set about creating a new kind of state. It was modelled on Zaporozhian practices, including electing the leader. According to the treaty signed with Poland, the Hetmanate's lands were cleared of Polish administrative and military authorities and replaced by Cossack equivalents. All Cossacks had the right to participate in making decisions, initially through the Sichova Rada (General Council), which was modelled on the council in the Zaporozhian Sich. A new administration was made up of members of the starshyna – educated landowning Cossack elites like Khmelnytsky. They were military men, so they organized their territory into military-administrative units called regimental districts (polky) and named them after town centres. Regimental commanders who had been elected by their regiments ruled these units. Gradually, the Hetmanate developed a central administration that consisted of various branches responsible for military, economic, legal, and other affairs, as well as a two-tiered electoral system for its General Military Council and Council of Officers.

As the Cossacks were busy setting up and running their new state, Poland continued to wage war with them. Khmelnytsky gradually realized that while he had successfully stood up to Poland and made some notable gains, the Cossacks were unlikely to succeed in the long run on their own. According to some historians, Khmelnytsky had visions of creating larger alliances. The Crimean Tatars and the Ottomans had been helpful at various stages of the war but proved unreliable as they sometimes switched sides. So Khmelnytsky turned to the only other option in the immediate region – Muscovy.

The Cossack leader entered into negotiations with the Muscovite tsar, and in 1654 they came to an agreement in Pereiaslav that remains controversial to this day. Ukrainian historians write that Khmelnytsky believed he was entering into a military alliance against Poland. Russian historians write that Khmelnytsky voluntarily subordinated himself, his Cossacks, and all Ukrainians to the authority of the tsar, driven by a desire to reunite with them. In reality, it was a clash of political cultures. The Cossacks had emerged out of the Polish realm, where nobles negotiated with the king and arrived at a mutual agreement, whereas Muscovy was an autocracy where the concept of rights did not exist. The tsar was a supreme ruler who did not swear oaths to his subjects. In the short run, this treaty solved Khmelnytsky's problems since he had achieved his goal of military support from Moscow. The Hetmanate was recognized by the tsar as a Cossack state, with an army of 60,000 and privileges for the elites. Khmelnytsky died three years later, not realizing that with the Pereiaslav Agreement, he had shifted the power balance in the region. By inviting Moscow to share power over Ukrainian lands, he strengthened their hand for future imperial expansion.

Ten years after Khmelnytsky's death, Muscovy and Poland went behind the Cossacks' backs. They signed the 1667 Treaty of Andrusovo, agreeing to divide their influence over Ukrainian lands into eastern and western parts using the Dnipro River, which runs roughly through the middle of the country, as the boundary. Kyiv remained on the Muscovite side while the Zaporozhian Sich was put under the two states' joint 'protection'. This meant there were separate hetmans for the two parts of Ukraine, and they did not always see eye to eye. These divisions were exploited by both Poland and Muscovy, and Cossack rights were gradually eroded. That said, they continued to be highly valued for their military skills. In 1683, Poland hired them to help in the defence of Vienna against the Ottoman Empire. Today, one can visit a monument in the city dedicated to the Cossacks that participated in this liberation. This state of affairs continued until a new Cossack hetman appeared on the scene, marking another turning point in Ukraine's history.

Ivan Mazepa (1639–1709) was a colourful figure whose escapades inspired the works of many European romantics. He was born in central Ukraine, had an international education, and served in the court of Polish kings in Warsaw. Legend has it he was chased out of the commonwealth after a scandalous affair with a married Polish noblewoman. Whether true or not, Mazepa did leave the Polish capital and headed east. He joined the service of the hetman east of the Dnipro River and was sent on numerous diplomatic missions, including to Moscow. Eventually, he was elected hetman himself and proceeded to build up the Hetmanate's economy, industry, culture, and education. He was also a strong supporter of the Orthodox Church. He tried to alleviate the difficult lives of peasants by reducing their obligations to the nobility, although in this he did not succeed. Later in life, at age sixty-five, he fell in love with his chancellor's sixteen-year-old daughter Motria, which caused serious tension between the two men. Motria chose her lover over her father.

Mazepa is remembered for many things, but most importantly for having tried to reunite Ukrainian territories and restore Cossack autonomy. He was an experienced diplomat and became a close confidante of Tsar Peter I, also known as Peter the Great. But at the same time, Mazepa maintained relations with leaders of other states. Watching as Cossack rights and independence were being increasingly eroded, he deliberated on how to reverse the trend and decided that the Cossacks needed to be removed from Moscow's sphere of control. Peter was busy engaging in imperial expansion plans. Hoping to gain control of the Baltic Sea, he had begun what is known as the Great Northern War. The tsar expected the Cossacks to help, but Mazepa had plans of his own. The hetman engaged in talks with Poland and Sweden and joined an anti-Muscovite coalition. His chancellor, still infuriated that Mazepa was living with his young daughter, tried to foil the plans and reported them to the tsar. But the Muscovite leader was so full of his own ideas and the firm belief that the Cossacks would serve him that he had the chancellor executed.

Things came to a head in 1709 near the central Ukrainian city of Poltava. Moscow troops and Cossacks who chose to fight on their side faced the Swedes and Cossacks loyal to Mazepa and soundly defeated them. Mazepa and his supporters had to flee, and he died in exile. Peter's troops destroyed Mazepa's capital along with all its 6,000 inhabitants. The tsar declared Mazepa a traitor and ordered the Church to place an anathema (curse) on him that remains intact to this day. But Mazepa's close associate Pylyp Orlyk continued the hetman's work and produced a constitution in 1710 to govern the Hetmanate. It was one of the world's earliest democratic constitutions. The original document, written in Latin, is in Sweden's National Archives. There is also a copy in Moscow.

The Poles and the Muscovites

The challenge the Cossacks ultimately faced was that they were caught in the crosshairs of historical forces. They had emerged when there was space, land, and opportunity to establish their own way of life, but by the eighteenth century, Europe began experiencing changes that worked against their interests. Globalization had begun, states were centralizing their governments, and empires were being reconfigured. The Cossacks were trying to preserve independence at a time when trends were moving in the opposite direction. Both the Poles and Ukrainians lost out in the process, while the Muscovites grew into one of the great powers of Europe.

The Khmelnytsky uprising and the wars that followed, as well as the creation of the Hetmanate and the division of Ukrainian lands between Poland and Muscovy, all took their toll on Poland. It reduced its grain profits and gradually its power. Poland's losses were Muscovy's gains. After achieving influence over eastern Ukrainian lands, the tsar allowed the Cossacks a degree of autonomy and used them as a military force to protect against Tatar attacks while pursuing his own agenda. Peter the I eventually won the Great Northern War in 1721, and that same year he changed his title to Emperor of All Russia. In this way, he continued to lay claim to the heritage of Kyivan Rus, even though Moscow had been a small provincial town during Kyiv's golden era, and his new imperial capital of St Petersburg, more than 1,000 miles from ancient Kyiv, had not existed at all. Cossack rights and powers continued to be eroded by both Poland and Russia.

Empress Catherine II, also known as Catherine the Great, dealt the final death blow to the Poles and Cossacks. The German princess who schemed her way to the top of the Russian Empire embarked on new colonization projects while corresponding with Voltaire about the Enlightenment. She waged war against the

Ottoman Turks and in 1783 annexed the Crimean Peninsula as well as the rest of the Tatar Khanate, which had become an Ottoman protectorate. This was when Crimea became part of the Russian Empire. The Crimean Tatar Khanate was renamed New Russia to create the illusion of virgin lands. Place names were changed, and local residents dispossessed in the classic style of settler colonialism that sought to obliterate the history of the people who had long lived there – much like what happened in North America or Australia. Large numbers of Tatars fled to Turkey, and in their historical narrative this period is known as the first Russian occupation. Centuries later, in 2014, Putin repeated this pattern when he annexed Crimea and began a stealth war against Ukraine in the country's south-east.

Back in the eighteenth century, after defeating the Ottomans and overtaking Crimea, Russia no longer needed the Zaporozhian Cossacks to protect the border region. Catherine abolished the Hetmanate and in 1775 ordered the destruction of the Zaporozhian Sich fortress. She forced the last hetman, Kyrylo Rozumovsky, to resign, gave him the title Field Marshal of Russian Imperial Army, and as historian Zenon Kohut wrote, this led to the imperial absorption of the Hetmanate. (Kohut, 1988).

Around the same time, Catherine worked to destroy Poland. She engaged in negotiations with Austria and Prussia and, through a series of treaties, wiped Poland off the map of Europe by 1795. In what is known as the Partitions of Poland, the three countries divided Poland's territories among themselves. Ukrainian lands were partitioned between the Austrian and Russian empires, and for the next few centuries, Ukrainians would be ruled by others. But new ideas began floating around Europe, and they would drift into Ukraine and cause ripples to the old order. The region's Cossack past would be an important part of that.

3 The Nation Builders

Introduction

Slava Ukraini means 'Glory to Ukraine'. In 2022, these words were being repeated all over the world as global leaders and ordinary people expressed their support for Ukraine following Russia's full-scale invasion. The phrase, in a slightly different form, was first written back in the nineteenth century by a poet called Taras Shevchenko, when Ukraine did not yet exist as a state. (In Shevchenko's version, it was *Slava Ukrainy*, or 'Glory of Ukraine'.) Ukrainians had their own language, history, and culture, but throughout the nineteenth and twentieth centuries, their lands were divided and ruled by others who tried to deny their existence. Ukraine's strategically important and resource-rich lands were at the centre of every great global confrontation of the modern era. But Ukrainians, Ukrainians wanted to govern themselves. So, they began writing about their nation and then fought to create their own state (Yekelchyk, 2007).

Shevchenko epitomized this struggle and became a leading light in Ukraine's nation-building movement. He was born into serfdom in 1814 on the estate of Baron Vasiliy Engelhardt, not far from Kyiv, which at the time was controlled by the Russian Empire. Serfdom had started to resemble slavery during this period, but the bright young serf caught his master's attention and was allowed to learn to read. He was also given drawing lessons. When Engelhardt took Shevchenko with him to the imperial capital, he snuck away to St Petersburg's Winter Garden to sketch. There he met other Ukrainians and Russian liberals who organized a fundraiser and purchased his freedom.

As a young boy, Shevchenko had grown up hearing stories about the Cossacks from his grandfather and he went on to write about them in his native Ukrainian language. He was such a gifted writer that his poetry laid the foundations of modern Ukrainian literature and Shevchenko became the national bard, Ukraine's Shakespeare if you will. Shevchenko also joined a secret society called the St Cyril and Methodius Brotherhood and together they formulated the first Ukrainian democratic platform that called for social and national liberation. These ideas challenged Russian imperial authority, and Shevchenko was arrested, imprisoned, exiled, and died an early death. But the Ukrainian idea continued.

Shevchenko's work was memorialized by Ukrainians, but little known internationally. Similarly, Ukraine rarely appears in mainstream history books covering this era. Those ruling over Ukrainians silenced their voices and presented their own colonial versions of their history to the world. They denied Ukrainians' nationhood, discredited their national movement as a foreign plot, and eliminated their leaders. Russian historians wrote history in a way that portrayed Kyiv as the cradle of Russian civilization and Ukrainians as 'Little Russians', which continues to shape the way many people think of Ukraine. Ukrainians challenged this historical disinformation war by writing about themselves and asserting their place in the world.

Ukraine's national movement emerged as part of the larger national awakening that swept through Europe and resulted in the creation of many new nation-states. The early nation builders were intellectuals, historians, and poets like Shevchenko. In the twentieth century, Ukraine found itself at the centre of new power struggles and wars, and Ukrainians became politicians and freedom fighters.

The Poets

The nineteenth and twentieth centuries were an era of tremendous global political, economic, and cultural changes. It was a time when the Age of Imperialism and the Age of Nationalism collided. Empires and monarchies dominated the world at the beginning of this period, and they were challenged by nationalism, democracy, liberalism, socialism, and fascism as people used these ideas to compete for power. Americans shook off British imperial rule and the French toppled their king with slogans of *Liberté, Égalité, Fraternite*. By 1918 all the Eastern European land empires collapsed, and new states appeared on the map of Europe. These revolutionary developments inspired people living on Ukrainian lands to believe that they too could change their future. They wanted the freedom to be who they were and to make their own choices.

Poets and intellectuals played a critical role in all national movements of the nineteenth century since they spread new ideas of change through their writing. Eastern Europe was ruled by three large empires: the Russian Empire, the Austrian Empire (later Austro-Hungarian), and the Ottoman Empire, and they exploited the lands and peoples they controlled. But the American and French revolutions showed that imperial monarchies could be challenged with the ideas of the Enlightenment – liberty, individual rights, and nation – and that power could be taken by the people. These ideas reached intellectuals throughout Europe during the Napoleonic Wars. When Napoleon's armies crossed the continent and reached as far as Moscow in 1812, Russian peasants joined French soldiers in looting the Russian imperial city, revealing their real attitude towards their imperial masters.

In the nineteenth century, Ukrainian lands were divided between the Austrian and Russian empires. The western part of these lands, less than a third of modern-day Ukraine, was under Austrian rule. Ukrainians made up only about 8 per cent of the Austrian Empire's total population, which consisted of more than twelve national groups. They lived in a province called Galicia, or *Halychyna* in Ukrainian, together with Poles and Jews. The Austrians organized their empire into provinces, roughly corresponding to national lands. In some cases, various national groups were grouped together, and they clashed against each other rather than challenge the authority of the imperial centre. The name of the province where Ukrainians lived came from the medieval town of Halych, which was once capital of a Kyivan Rus principality. In the Austrian era, more than 45 per cent of Halychyna's population was Polish, while 43 per cent were Ukrainians, 11 per cent Jews, and the remaining 1 per cent Germans and other ethnic groups (Magocsi, 2010). But Poles remained dominant in political, social, and cultural life, as they had been for centuries, and this led to constant tensions with Ukrainians determined to make their own decisions.

The larger portion of Ukrainian lands, those in central, southern, and eastern Ukraine, were part of the Russian Empire. After Catherine II abolished the Cossack Hetmanate in 1764, these lands lost their separate status and self-rule.

They were blended into the rest of the empire as nine out of thirty-five provinces (*gubernias* in Russian) and were referred to as 'South Russia'. The Russian Empire was a multinational state at this time, with over 190 different ethnic groups living within its borders. Russians made up the largest group, at 44 per cent of the population; Ukrainians the second largest at 18 per cent, followed by Poles (6 per cent), Belarusians (5 per cent), and Jews (4 per cent).

In both the Russian and Austrian empires most people were peasants. That meant they were serfs, peasants tied to the land. By the time Shevchenko was born, serfdom in the Russian Empire resembled slavery, with landlords able to buy and sell serfs as if they were chattel. The other classes (estates) were townspeople, clergy, and the nobility. Much of what had earlier been Ukrainian nobility had assimilated into the new imperial realities to preserve their status and power.

But the waves of nationalism sweeping through Europe also came to Ukraine. Intellectuals and clergy in both empires started to write about Ukraine and its culture, traditions, and history in their native language, calling themselves Ukrainians (Bilenky, 2012). The naming issue surrounding the country is important but complicated because it relates to larger issues and often causes confusion. Until the nineteenth century, most people did not think of themselves in terms of nations; they were described by the states or empires in which they lived. When the Ukrainian national movement emerged, many Ukrainians were living in what was then the Russian Empire. They considered themselves descendants of the people of Kyivan Rus, but a variant of that name, Russia, had been adopted by Muscovy. To make it clear that they were a separate nation, intellectuals chose the word Ukraine (*Ukrania, Oukraina*), which has often been translated as borderland. The term dates back to the Kyivan Rus era and was used in Cossack times to describe Cossack lands. Centuries later, it was adopted by people like Shevchenko living in what is today Ukraine. In the Austrian Empire, the name was less of an issue since Ukrainians living there were not being blurred with Austrians or Poles. They continued to call themselves the people of Rus (*Rusyny*, translated into English as Ruthenians or Rusyns) well into the early twentieth century while sharing the same language as the people calling themselves Ukrainians in the Russian Empire. Other nations divided among the different empires, for example, the Poles, whose lands had been split between Russia, Austria, and Prussia, also had language as a common element of their identity.

Language was an important part of how nations defined themselves then, with literature and the written word playing an integral role in uniting people. It helped the nation-building process, particularly among ethnic groups living within larger empires, since it helped standardize a national language (Hroch, 1996). Modern Ukrainian literature began appearing in the early part of this era. The first known work in modern Ukrainian was published in 1798. It was written by Ivan Kotliarevsky, a Latin-educated tutor from Poltava in central Ukraine, which was then part of the Russian Empire. Although Kotliarevsky appears serious in portraits, with a high collar and white tie, he clearly had a sense of humour. He wrote a satirical poem loosely based on Virgil's classic *Aeneid*, calling his version *Eneida*. Its heroes were not Trojans but Zaporozhian Cossacks. At the time, the memory of the Cossacks was still very much alive, the poem became popular, and although the first parts were published without Kotliarevsky's permission, he became famous. In western Ukraine, a trio of theology students published the first known Ukrainian-language literature in the 1830s. Markian Shashkevych, Yakiv Holovatsky, and Ivan Vahylevych became interested in folklore, history, and doing general good for their people. They established a literary group called the *Ruska Triitsia* (Ruthenian Triad) and started to publish their works in Ukrainian. Not all Ukrainians at this time were choosing to write in their own language. Shevchenko's contemporary and neighbour, Mykola Hohol, chose to write in Russian and became world renowned as Nikolai Gogol, the Russian novelist and playwright.

Works by poets and writers were part of larger changes that were happening in Europe. The Industrial Revolution, the spread of literacy, and growing international trade all changed the way people lived and thought about their lives. This challenged the status quo where imperial monarchies often held absolute power. In 1848–9 a series of revolutions swept through Europe known as the Springtime of Nations. People in France, Ireland, Spain, Denmark, Sweden, Belgium, the Italian and German states, as well as many other countries demanded that their democratic, liberal, and national rights be recognized. These revolutions came to the Austrian Empire too. Many nations, including Ukrainians, demanded greater autonomy or independence. Ukrainians created the Supreme Ruthenian (Ukrainian) Council, the first legal Ukrainian political organization in modern times. They petitioned for their own province, education in Ukrainian, equal rights for their clergy, and better conditions for the peasantry. When faced with revolution, Austria agreed to some concessions. It eventually created a dual monarchy, established a parliament, allowed the various national groups to create political parties, put forth their political demands, and have education in their own languages, as well as allowing cultural and religious freedoms. The empire began to see itself as multinational or, as historian Timothy Snyder (2022) said, an early vision of a European Union.

Today, visitors to Vienna can visit the old parliament building and see where the first Ukrainian political parties sat. They never got their own province but did gain political representation, were able to use their own language, teach their children and publish in it, worship in their own traditions, and basically be Ukrainian, developing their national identity without having much political power.

The Historians

Things were dramatically different for Ukrainians living in the Russian Empire. While Austria recognized the various nations living within its borders and gave them some rights, the Russian Empire was going in the opposite direction – oppression. The tsar ruled with absolute power and rejected 'foreign ideas' of rights. How he went about doing this has shaped mental maps of Russia and Ukraine into the present. Many people today continue to think of the Russian Empire, the USSR, and the Russian Federation as 'Russia' rather than the multinational entities they actually were and, in the case of the Russian Federation, still are.

History is an important part of identity. During the rise of nationalism in the nineteenth century many nations began to write their histories, their origin stories explaining who they were, where they came from, and teaching that to their children and the world. The Russian Empire took a different approach. It wrote its history as an imperial one. Tsar Alexander I asked his friend Nikolai Karamzin, historian and poet, to write an official history of the Russian Empire. Karamzin devoted the rest of his life to producing the twelve-volume *History of the Russian State* (1816–29). It was, in effect, an apologia for Russian autocracy, arguing that the Russian Empire was the direct and only successor to Kyivan Rus, and that Kyiv was the cradle of Russian civilization. Although the writing of history is often political (MacMillan, 2008), the way history is written has changed over time (Carr, 1986). Yet this imperial version of history would continue, be expanded upon by other Russian historians, successfully exported, and continue to be taught throughout the world (Zayarnyuk, 2022).

The image of a united Russia was reinforced in the 1830s when the tsar's education minister Sergey Uvarov proposed the idea that Russian identity was composed of three pillars: Orthodoxy, autocracy, and nationality. This became the empire's official ideology. It merged the ideas of nation and empire into one, suggesting that the Russian Empire was one nation, and that the people within it were Russian, Orthodox, and supported autocracy, which in effect meant the absolute rule of the tsar. This caused problems for nations like Ukrainians because it denied their separate existence. It also created a long-term conundrum for Russians because they never developed a Russian national identity that was not imperial (Tolz, 2001).

While the Russian imperial leaders were attempting to construct a common identity, Ukrainians were trying to decolonize this way of thinking by writing their own history. The first history appeared sometime in the early nineteenth century by an unknown author and was called *Istoriia Rusov* ('The History of the Rus People'). The story began in Kyivan Rus and then went on to describe the Lithuanian, Polish, and Cossack periods. In other words, it outlined the historical developments on Ukrainian lands before colonization by Muscovy. This laid the foundations for Ukraine's history as a separate nation.

Mykhailo Hrushevsky, a bearded, bespectacled historian, later expanded this history into a ten-volume study called *History of Ukraine-Rus (1891–1934)*. His detailed archival research showed that Ukrainian and Russian historical developments were distinctly different up to the seventeenth century. But his work was supressed by the authorities. He died under suspicious circumstances in 1934 and his work did not reach large international audiences – they continued reading the Russian version of history. Many Ukrainian historians adopted Hrushevsky's framework and developed his ideas further. In the late twentieth and early twenty-first centuries, the entire magnum opus was translated into English and published by the Canadian Institute of Ukrainian Studies under the direction of historian Frank Sysyn and is now widely available. Today, many consider Hrushevsky the father of Ukrainian history, and his face is on the country's 50-hryvnia banknote.

Part of the reason the Russian Empire was constructing this common identity was to project an image of power. It was the largest country in Europe and Asia but lagged far behind in terms of economic output, literacy levels, industrialization, trade, and efficiency. Although it appeared militarily strong, the empire lost the 1853–6 Crimean War virtually in its own backyard because of its backwardness. The country's elites realized that reforms were needed, but they were difficult to implement in the authoritarian system. When in 1861 the tsar finally abolished serfdom, it was intended to improve the agricultural sector by giving peasants their freedom, but the way it was conducted did not leave the peasants much better off and output did not markedly improve.

Ukraine was important to the Russian Empire for several reasons, including identity, economics, and its strategic location. By tracing the empire's history back to Kyiv, which was more ancient than Moscow, a story was constructed that the Ukrainian lands had always been Russian and therefore the empire had an inherent right to rule them. Ukraine was also economically important to the empire. In the mid-1800s, Ukrainians comprised only 18 per cent of the population but Ukrainian lands accounted for 75 per cent of the empire's exports. The country's fertile soil produced high-quality grain that the empire sold abroad – Ukraine was the 'breadbasket of Europe'. One of the world's largest coal deposits was discovered in Ukraine's south-eastern Donbas region, turning it into a booming industrial heartland that attracted foreign investment and waves of migrants from Russia. Strategically, by controlling Ukrainian lands, the Russian Empire stretched well into Eastern Europe. The southern coast, the port of Odesa, and the Crimean Peninsula gave the empire strategic access to the Mediterranean through the Black Sea. As British scholar Halford Mackinder later wrote in 1919, whoever controlled the east European heartland, meaning Ukraine and Poland, could rule the world.

As a result, the Ukrainian nation builders posed a very real threat to the Russian imperial project. The empire responded by calling them 'Little Russians', arresting their intellectuals and leaders, prohibiting their works, and attempting to destroy their language. In 1863, a secret decree called the Valuev Circular declared that the Ukrainian language 'does not exist, has never existed, and never would exist'. A few years later, the 1876 Ems decree went even further, prohibiting the printing and distribution of what it called 'Ukrainophile propaganda in the southern gubernias of Russia'. Ukrainians got around these bans by sending their works to their colleagues in the Austrian Empire and publishing them there.

The oppressive nature of the Russian Empire and the poor living conditions of most of its population led to rising discontent. Since the empire outlawed any political activity, secret revolutionary groups began to form and advocate for change; however they held different views on how that change should look. Socialist ideas became quite popular in addition to national ones. When in 1904–5 Russia lost another war, this time against Japan, massive social discontent erupted into a 1905 revolution and demands for change. At first, Tsar Nicholas II responded with the use of force, but eventually he agreed to some concessions: reforms were promised, a constitution was drafted, political parties were finally allowed, including Ukrainian ones, and a parliament (called the Duma) was created.

Almost a decade later, in 1914, World War I began, which pitted Austria and Russia against each other. Ukrainians were drafted to serve in both imperial armies, which forced them into the position that they were fighting against each other for causes that were not their own. As the war dragged on, the two empires faced growing domestic pressures. Combined with the burden of war, they found it increasingly hard to govern. The Russian Empire collapsed in 1917, and Austri-Hungary followed in 1918. As the empires were falling apart, Ukrainians and other nations saw an opportunity to rid themselves of imperial rule. They seized it and began creating their own nation-states.

Politicians and Freedom Fighters

The historian Mykhailo Hrushevsky was busy in his library writing when the Russian Revolution began in the spring of 1917. He was in exile in Moscow, but in Kyiv, Ukrainian political activists moved quickly to organize Ukraine's first modern state. A few days after the tsar abdicated, various Ukrainian organizations and parties gathered in Kyiv. On 17 March, they established a Central Rada (Central Council/Tsentralna Rada), declared themselves the revolutionary parliament of Ukraine, and elected Hrushevsky as their chairman. They adopted the word *Rada* from the Cossack era, raised the blue and yellow Ukrainian flag, issued a declaration to the Ukrainian people, called an election, started planning land reforms, and created an army. By autumn, they called themselves the Ukrainian National Republic and declared they wanted to live in peace and harmony with their neighbours but were prepared to defend themselves.

When the Austrian Empire collapsed a year later, in 1918, Ukrainian elites living there proclaimed their own republic: the Western Ukrainian People's Republic. They took control of the Ukrainian Sich Riflemen, a Ukrainian unit within the Austrian army, and in early 1919 joined forces with their fellow compatriots in Kyiv to establish a unified Ukrainian state and army. On 22 January 1919, the Treaty of Unity was signed merging western and eastern Ukraine into one state. This date, known as Ukrainian Unity Day, continues to be celebrated in modern Ukraine. Other nations in the former empires pursued similar state-building initiatives.

As Ukrainians were busy trying to build their own state, their lands yet again became a battleground. Once more, foreign powers wanted to gain control over their abundant resources and strategic location, and they were invaded from all sides. As historian Dominic Lieven wrote: 'As much as anything, World War I turned on the fate of Ukraine' (Lieven, 2015, p. 1). This would remain the case throughout the twentieth century. Germany dreamt of creating a Mitteleuropa that stretched through Ukraine all the way to the Caucasus. The Bolsheviks wanted a world revolution but instead recreated the old Russian Eurasian empire under communist rule. Meanwhile, the newly recreated Poland imagined it could restore its old commonwealth borders. All three powers laid claim to Ukrainian lands and invaded them. From 1917 to 1921, Ukrainians fought a series of wars against various invaders. They went through several governments that one after another declared independence in their effort to create a Ukrainian state.

To say that Ukrainian elites faced tremendous challenges in their effort to achieve their statehood would be an understatement. They were being attacked by armies from all sides while having no experience in governing, few resources at their disposal, and limited levers of power. What's more, they had different visions of what their state should look like and who their main enemies were. Some were socialists who wanted to cooperate with the Bolsheviks, others were conservatives who felt Germany was a better ally, while western Ukrainians feared the Poles. Not everyone from Ukraine even shared the national idea. Lev Davidovich Bronstein, known to the world as Leon Trotsky, was born to a wealthy Ukrainian-Jewish family in Yanovka in central Ukraine. He became a leading Bolshevik and founder of the Red Army that invaded Ukraine in 1919.

Yet despite their differences, many Ukrainian leaders shared a European, democratic, inclusive vision. The Ukrainian National Republic printed its declaration of independence in four languages: Ukrainian, Russian, Polish, and Yiddish. They sent a delegation to the Paris Peace Conference to ask for international recognition and, even though they were denied this recognition, they did their best to defend their land.

Symon Petliura became a key figure during this period. He had been a journalist and then political leader who engaged in Ukrainian revolutionary activities and set up and led the Ukrainian People's Army. Men and women signed up, prepared to fight and die for Ukraine, but they were often badly outnumbered. For example, at the January 1918 Battle of Kruty a 4,000-strong Bolshevik army was advancing on Kyiv and Ukrainians could only assemble about 500 soldiers, mainly cadets, to defend themselves. They managed to hold off the invaders long enough for their government to sign the Brest-Litovsk Treaty with Germany and Austria, but about half of the young soldiers were killed. In Ukrainian culture, they were later immortalized as heroes. By contrast, the Russian writer Mikhail Bulgakov, who lived in Kyiv through these events, dismissively depicted Petliura and the Ukrainian Army as 'rabble' in his famous novel *The White Guard*.

Amid all the warfare, many innocent people were killed, particularly Jews who were targeted by all armies, including Ukrainian forces. The Ukrainian National Republic had promised Jews full equality and autonomy. The Jewish lawyer Arnold Margolin was appointed as its deputy minister of foreign affairs and capital punishment was introduced for carrying out pogroms. Yet the UNR could not guarantee their safety and Petliura was demonized as an anti-Semite. Once Ukrainians were defeated, he ended up having to flee the country and was later assassinated in Paris.

Crimean Tatars also faced a harsh fate during this time. They set up their own Crimean People's Republic in late 1917 but a few months later Bolshevik forces invaded. They executed the Crimean Tatar president Noman Çelebicihan, threw his body into the Black Sea, and later incorporated the peninsula into the Russian Federation as an autonomous republic.

When peace finally came in 1921, it was not the one Ukrainians had envisioned when they shouted *Slava Ukraini!* going into battle. Despite their efforts, they failed to secure their statehood and Ukrainian lands were once again divided, roughly along the same lines as before but this time among four newly created states: the USSR, Poland, Romania, and Czechoslovakia. Ukrainian leaders went into exile where they continued to seek support for their independence project, in part through cultural diplomacy. Ukrainian composer Mykola Leontovych's 'Shchedryk' was performed at New York's Carnegie Hall in 1922. It became internationally loved as the 'Carol of the Bells' but few knew of the song's Ukrainian origins. Leontovych was killed by the Soviet secret police, and while his music survived, he was not recognized as the composer for decades. In 2022, 'Shchedryk' was performed once again at Carnegie Hall, this time identified as Leontovych's work.

Throughout the interwar years, the Ukrainian national idea lived on in the new realities. Ukrainian territory that had been part of the Russian Empire was incorporated into the Soviet Union, while most of western Ukraine ended up in the newly reconstituted Poland, with small areas absorbed into Romania and Czechoslovakia. In the east, Vladimir Lenin, the first head of the Soviet state, understood that controlling Ukraine was key to his Bolshevik project, and reportedly said: 'If we lose Ukraine, we lose our head.' Rather than continuing to fight against Ukrainian national sentiment, the Soviet leader decided to try and co-opt it. He believed that nationalism would gradually disappear as people embraced the idea of communism. So the new Bolshevik state was set up as a federation, and the Ukrainians were given their own republic, the Ukrainian Socialist Soviet Republic within the Union of Soviet Socialist Republics (USSR). The Communist Party held power, but Ukrainians and other nations were given their own republics and allowed to use their national languages in what historian Terry Martin (2001) called an Affirmative Action Empire. Yet nationalism did not disappear. Ukrainians and other nations within the USSR wanted more political rights.

Joseph Stalin, a Russified Bolshevik from Georgia, was sent to a seminary as a child, but his ecclesiastical start did not stop him from turning into one of the twentieth century's worst dictators. After Lenin's premature death, he became the new Soviet leader and decided to use force against this desire for greater national political rights. Stalin imposed revolution from above and a reign of terror against society in all spheres, including to eliminate nationalism. The results were disastrous for Ukrainians. In effect he perpetrated genocide against Ukrainians, considering them a great threat. Intellectuals and clergy were arrested and sent to the Gulag and millions of farmers were starved to death in an artificially created famine known as the 1932–3 Holodomor. Stalin said his policies of rapid industrialization and forcible collectivization of agriculture were needed for the USSR to survive. But the Polish-Jewish lawyer Raphael Lemkin's observations of Stalin's assault on the Ukrainian countryside, intelligentsia, and clergy led him to coin the term genocide. Lemkin's ideas were instrumental in the drafting of the 1948 United Nations Convention on Genocide.

In western Ukraine, national and other minority rights were initially respected by Czechoslovakia, and to a lesser degree by Poland and Romania. These countries had all agreed to respect minority rights in a series of international treaties they signed with the League of Nations when they were recognized as new states. Ukrainians were allowed to create political parties, participate in the democratic process, and develop their cultural, religious, and civic lives as Ukrainians. Then things changed. A series of economic and political crises hit. Democratic beliefs started to be squeezed out by extremist ideologies, with some countries in Europe taking a sharp turn to the right. Interwar Germany is the best-known example, but similar developments were occurring in Eastern Europe where new/old states like Poland were beginning to oppress their minorities. Liberal Ukrainians continued trying to work according to democratic principles, but more radical Ukrainians created the Organization of Ukrainian Nationalists (OUN) and began advocating an extreme form of nationalism. They adopted a modified version of Shevchenko's *Slava Ukrainy* as their official slogan. There are no reliable statistics on OUN's membership, but estimates indicate there were as many as 20,000 members in 1939.

Then World War II broke out, and Ukrainians found themselves in the crosshairs of Europe's most brutal dictators – Hitler and Stalin. Both men wanted to control Ukraine. Hitler planned to colonize the country and use it as living space, *Lebensraum*, for Germans. He viewed Ukrainians as subhuman *Untermenschen*; they were to be enslaved and their land taken. Stalin wanted to edge further into Eastern Europe and expand his control over western parts of Ukraine. But Ukrainians had plans of their own. As war raged and borders once again shifted, they saw another opportunity to create their own state.

Stepan Bandera was the son of a priest who became leader of the radical branch of OUN. The rather petite man is, like many Ukrainian leaders, considered a hero by some and a villain by others. Throughout his life he was imprisoned by the Poles then Nazis and assassinated by a KGB agent. Bandera became involved with the nationalists in the 1930s and quickly moved up the ranks. He considered both Poland and the Soviet Union enemies of the Ukrainian people and was prepared to work with the enemies of Ukraine's enemies, including Nazi Germany, to achieve the goal of independence.

When war erupted the younger members of OUN split from the older conservatives and elected Bandera as their leader. They became known as Banderites, or OUN-B. When the German Army marched into Ukraine, Bandera's followers went with them and on 30 June 1941 proclaimed an independent Ukrainian state. The Germans condemned the move and Bandera was promptly detained. He spent much of the rest of the war under German arrest or in concentration camps. But OUN members continued their quest for independence. A partisan military force called the Ukrainian Insurgent Army (UPA) sprang up, numbering between 25,000 and 40,000 members at its height. For the duration of the war, OUN and UPA continued trying to create an independent Ukrainian state. They fought on many fronts, against the Soviet, German, and Polish armies, and at times against civilian populations, including Poles, Jews, and also fellow Ukrainians.

Ukrainian lands were also a major site of the Holocaust. Before Germany invaded in 1941, they were home to one of the largest Jewish populations in Europe. By the end of the war, an estimated two out of three Ukrainian Jews had been murdered. The 1941 Babyn Yar massacre in Kyiv was one of the largest mass killings of Jews in Nazi-occupied Europe. On 29–30 September, more than 33,000 Jews were shot and killed in a ravine on the outskirts of the city. Afterwards, Soviet authorities systematically denied that Jews had been singled out as targets of Nazi atrocities.

While the Holocaust in Ukraine has been well studied, much less is known about the ethnic cleansing Stalin perpetrated against the Crimean Tatars. Although many Crimean Tatars were fighting in the Red Army, Stalin accused them of being Nazi collaborators and had the entire nation deported in cattle cars to Central Asia in a secret special operation that took place on 18–20 May 1944. Large numbers died along the way, and tens of thousands subsequently perished due to the harsh exile conditions in the east.

The war in Europe formally ended in May 1945, and borders changed once again. The USSR expanded its territory to control even more than the old Russian imperial lands, including parts of western Ukraine that had never been under Russian rule, as well as Belarus and the Baltic states. In other words, much of what Mackinder had called the Eastern European heartland. From there, Stalin was able to expand his influence deeper into the European continent. Combined with the country's nuclear arsenal, this led to the USSR becoming a world superpower. Ironically, it was Stalin who united most Ukrainian ethnolinguistic lands into one territory – a Soviet republic that would go on to gain its independence and become modern Ukraine. Six years of World War II devastated Ukraine since that is where some of the continent's heaviest fighting had occurred. Ukraine suffered some of the highest casualty rates of the war (Edele, 2021), and much of its infrastructure was destroyed. Then in 1946, it experienced a post-war famine, and Stalin unleashed yet another wave of repression as the Cold War began.

In western Ukraine, which had just been incorporated into the USSR, the Ukrainian nationalist movement continued fighting against Soviet rule.

The UPA increasingly switched to guerrilla tactics, and those who went abroad made contact with Western intelligence agencies. Together they launched a 'Parachute Scheme', which could be made into a wonderful Cold War movie: OUN members were dropped by parachute into western Ukraine where the UPA was still actively operating. Their mission was to weaken Soviet rule by bolstering the Ukrainian resistance and, more importantly, to collect intelligence for the West. This scheme failed completely since the KGB had infiltrated the British spy agency MI5. The Cambridge-educated Kim Philby informed his Moscow handlers of the times and locations of the parachute drops. Ukrainians were promptly picked up, arrested, and interrogated. Some of them broke under torture and started working for the KGB, feeding false information to the West.

The USSR also set about eliminating Ukrainian nationalist leaders. The commander of the UPA, Roman Shukhevych, was killed in a shootout with Interior Ministry troops in 1950. Many OUN–UPA members were arrested and sent to the Soviet Gulag. Others went abroad but that did not guarantee their safety. In 1959, Bandera was killed in Munich by a KGB assassin with a poison gun. The extraordinary technique would later inspire Ian Fleming's James Bond novel *The Man with the Golden Gun* (Plokhii, 2016). Stalin launched a major propaganda campaign to discredit Ukrainian nationalism, demonize Bandera, and portray him and all Ukrainian nationalists as Nazis. Decades later, Putin would borrow from the same playbook and call all Ukrainian elites Nazis.

Things changed briefly following Stalin's death in 1953. Nikita Khrushchev, a short bald man best known for bringing the world to the brink of nuclear war during the Cuban Missile Crisis, became the new Soviet leader. He had earlier governed in Ukraine, and once in Moscow he transferred Crimea to the Ukrainian Republic. He also loosened restrictions on society in a policy of 'de-Stalinization', and a new wave of independent-minded intellectuals and writers sprang up across the republics. In Ukraine, they criticized Soviet authorities for not adhering to their own constitution which guaranteed language and cultural rights – instead, they had intensified Russification and falsified history. But in 1964, Khrushchev was deposed in a peaceful coup, and the trio that replaced him soon started cracking down with new restrictive measures. Leonid Brezhnev, who gradually took the lead, went on to rule the Soviet Union for eighteen years. Living standards rose but at the same time dissent was suppressed. Countless Ukrainians were arrested, and they became the largest percentage of political prisoners in the Gulag. Some died in the harsh labour camps, but others like Viacheslav Chornovil and Levko Lukianenko survived and would play a key role in the next phase of Ukraine's history.

During the years that followed, dreams of independence and statehood did not disappear in Ukraine, but they became submerged. Then in 1985, Mikhail

Gorbachev became the General Secretary of the Communist Party and the Soviet Union's new leader. He would introduce changes that once again created an opening for Ukrainians to pursue their dream of statehood.

4 The State Builders

Introduction

And then the day came. On 24 August 1991 Ukraine declared independence. Over 90 per cent of the population supported this in a referendum held on 1 December and Ukraine became a recognized member of the international community. After centuries of being divided and ruled by others and multiple attempts to establish their own state, Ukrainians at long last were able to govern themselves. The country was larger than France, had a diverse population of 52 million, and the world's third biggest nuclear arsenal. When Ukraine embarked on statehood, it was completely integrated into a decaying Soviet economy and few in the world had ever heard of Ukraine. Within a few decades, the country turned its economy around, built the cornerstones of democracy, and welcomed in the international community. It also became a popular European tourist destination, and won international tournaments – from the Olympics to the Eurovision Song Contest to prestigious math competitions.

Ukrainians elected the fifty-seven-year-old silver-haired Leonid Kravchuk as their first president on 1 December, the same day the country held its independence referendum. Kravchuk was from the Rivne Region in western Ukraine and had worked his way up the Communist Party hierarchy fighting Ukrainian 'bourgeois nationalism'. Following independence, he became Ukraine's modern state builder. As his contemporary Volodymyr Filenko said, at the crucial moment, '*Volyniaka peremih komuniaku v Kravchuky (Волиняка переміг комуняку в Кравчуку)*' (Collapse, 2021, Episode 6). This apt, witty phrase is impossible to translate with Filenko's panache, but it basically means that when push came to shove, local identity proved stronger than communist ideology.

The push, meaning tensions within the USSR, was coming from many directions, and in 1991 Ukraine dealt the shove, the death blow to the 'Last Empire', as Harvard historian Serhii Plokhii (2014) called the Soviet Union. Ukraine was aptly described by Sherman Garnett (1997) as the 'Keystone in the Arch'. When the keystone left, the entire arch collapsed, leaving Ukraine free to redefine itself and rejoin Europe, if it so chose.

What many underestimated at the time was the reaction in Moscow. Ukraine had gained its statehood while Russia had lost its empire. Losing control over Ukraine threatened Russia's entire identity, its foundation myth. Kyiv was now the capital of an independent Ukraine, the city that Russians had for centuries been taught was the cradle of their civilization. Ukraine had decolonized; where did this leave Russia? Equally important was that Poland immediately allied itself with Ukraine – it was the first country to formally recognize Ukraine's independence, beating Canada by just hours. Centuries of antagonism were put aside, and a new relationship began, not unlike that between France and Germany following World War II. Both Poland and Ukraine were celebrating their return to Europe, while Russia was left trying to redefine itself. It faced an important choice, and one in which Ukraine played a central role. As Zbigniew Brzezinski wrote in 1994: 'It cannot be stressed enough that without Ukraine, Russia ceases to be an empire, but with Ukraine suborned and then subordinated, Russia automatically becomes an empire.'

The disintegration of an empire is a process, not an event. It began well before 1991, and its legacy continues to linger. Many factors led to the USSR's implosion, which began with Gorbachev's reforms in the mid-1980s and with the explosion at Chornobyl, the worst nuclear disaster in history. It happened on Ukrainian territory and Soviet authorities initially tried covering it up. But the Communist Party could not contain the nuclear fallout from the explosion and when Sweden began reporting elevated levels of radiation in Europe, Gorbachev decided to admit the accident. Once Ukrainians learned that the Communist Party had initially suppressed the story, exposed them and their children to radiation while secretly evacuating their own families, discontent started bubbling up to the surface. The genie was out of the bottle. Long-standing grievances began being aired, the suppressed national question among them. Groups began appearing advocating environmental protection and were soon followed by those demanding better Ukrainian language and cultural rights and eventually making political demands.

The Democrats

In the spring of 1989, Maria Burmaka was a nineteen-year-old student in Kharkiv, Ukraine's second-largest city and one that was predominantly Russian speaking. She heard about a music festival in Chernivsti in western Ukraine, packed her guitar, and hopped on a train. Chervona Ruta was the first Ukrainian rock festival in the country, and musicians from all over the country came together to sing revolutionary songs in Ukrainian. Police presence was heavy and anyone carrying the banned blue and yellow Ukrainian national flag was beaten or arrested. Maria was the youngest musician there, but together with other performers, she spoke out openly against police brutality while on stage. Years later, she said in an interview, 'I was young, I didn't realize how dangerous it was to speak out.' Her song about rising up and breaking chains of oppression caught the judges' attention. Maria won second prize in the singer-songwriter category and launched her musical career.

That same year, democratically minded Ukrainians, Russians, Armenians, Jews, and others joined forces to form a political organization they called Rukh, a movement for restructuring Ukraine. Luck was on their side when a year later Gorbachev repealed Article 6 of the Soviet constitution, which had given the Communist Party a monopoly on political power. That meant Rukh, or any other organization, could field candidates in elections. They did and Rukh members were elected to parliament in 1990. They then joined other democratically minded MPs and formed an opposition bloc called the National Council (Narodna Rada), once again adopting the historic word *Rada*. They were still a minority, 125 out of 450 MPs, so the new opposition could not make any political decisions. But they were powerful orators, and since the parliamentary proceedings were broadcast nationally, they gained access to the eyes and ears of the entire nation. They used this to their advantage, arguing against Gorbachev's proposed New Union Treaty.

On 19 August 1991, hardliners in Moscow staged a coup. They arrested Gorbachev and set out to reverse his reforms. They failed. Ukraine's parliament quickly convened an emergency session for 24 August, where the Narodna Rada tabled a motion for Ukraine to declare independence, which was legal under the Soviet constitution. The dramatic events of that day have been brilliantly captured in a documentary series called *Collapse: How Ukrainians Destroyed the Evil Empire* (2021). The communist majority eventually joined the democratic opposition and overwhelmingly voted for Ukrainian independence. Moscow panicked, despite all the turmoil in their capital. Russian president Boris Yeltsin's press secretary issued a statement that the borders with Ukraine needed to be revised, and on 28 August, a special delegation was despatched to Kyiv to deal with the 'emergency situation'. Yury Shcherbak, a Ukrainian MP who was on that plane, later described how during the flight the delegation members were nervous, drinking, and asking each other incredulously, 'What had those "khakhly" done?' (*Collapse*, Episode 7). *Khakhly* is a pejorative term Russians use for Ukrainians. For centuries, Russians had been taught that Ukrainians were their little brothers, that Kyiv was the cradle of their civilization, and that Ukrainian nationalism was a foreign plot to weaken Russia. And here Ukrainians had voted to leave the empire!

Kravchuk and others managed to smooth over the situation for the time being, but the Russia question would loom large over Ukraine as it embarked on what scholars have called its massive quadruple transition. Like other post-communist countries, Ukraine needed to democratize, develop a market economy and civil society, and also consolidate a nation-state. But there was no roadmap; this had never been done. Few in Ukraine understood what a market economy was, and they did not control the main levers of power in their own country. Moscow controlled the military, including its nuclear arsenal, the money supply, media communications, and the entire economy. For the first few years, Ukraine's focus was on survival, taking control of its own affairs, building its armed forces, and establishing itself in the international community.

The Stabilizers and Consolidators

Declaring independence and consolidating statehood are not the same thing. The first few years of independence were incredibly difficult for Ukraine, and many commentators at the time were sceptical the country would survive. The economy plummeted, poverty skyrocketed, and tensions with its northern neighbour increased. Russia refused to recognize Ukraine's borders and made claims on the Black Sea Fleet harboured in Crimea. International aid was not forthcoming since Ukraine was refusing to transfer the nuclear weapons on its territory to Russia. The state apparatus was inadequate, and many basic components simply did not exist. For example, Russia had taken over all the old Soviet embassies, so Ukraine had to set up its own. In 1991, the only international diplomatic representation the country had was the seat at the United Nations it inherited from the Ukrainian SSR.

To top things off, there was little political unity. Kravchuk had left the Communist Party but the democrats did not trust him, so he had no power base and this made it difficult for him to govern. The charismatic former political prisoner and Rukh leader Viacheslav Chornovil had been his primary opponent in the presidential race and continued to oppose him on many issues. Where they did agree was on the need to create a Ukrainian army and look for alternative energy supplies to reduce dependency on Russia. One of the first steps Ukraine took after declaring independence was to take charge of all military units and equipment stationed on its territory, including nuclear weapons. It also established its own Defence Ministry, on 24 September 1991. Ukrainians had learned from 1917 that without a strong army, they would not survive. Then on 6 December 1991, a Ukrainian delegation flew to Baku to negotiate an oil deal with Azerbaijan.

While this represented a good start, by 1993 all the post-Soviet states were seriously struggling, and economic problems led to political crises. Things that year came to a head in both Ukraine and Russia, but with very different outcomes. Ukraine's prime minister resigned, and early parliamentary and presidential elections were called for the following year. The former prime minister Leonid Kuchma ran against the incumbent Kravchuk and soundly defeated him. Kravchuk calmly stepped aside. This smooth transition of power was touted as an important step in the consolidation of Ukraine's democracy. The Communist Party won the largest number of seats in parliament, setting them on a collision course with the reform-minded new president. In Russia, President Boris Yeltsin also found himself battling with his country's legislatures, the Congress of People's Deputies and the Supreme Soviet. But rather than stepping down, he dissolved both chambers on 21 September 1993. They refused to comply, people took to the streets, and violence erupted. Yeltsin called the protestors 'fascist-communists' and ordered the army to storm the Russian White House where the MPs sat. Once they were chased out of the burnt building and Yeltsin revised the constitution to give himself, as president, more power, he continued to govern Russia until resigning in 1999.

In Ukraine, the new president Leonid Kuchma took power in 1994. The ginger-haired Kuchma was born in Polissia, the part of northern Ukraine bordering Russia and Belarus. By his own admission, he never thought much about national identity in his youth, and had probably never heard of the Chervona Ruta music festival. He grew up to become the director of the largest missile factory in the USSR, Iuzhmash, located in what was then called Dnipropetrovsk in central Ukraine. Unsurprisingly, he ran for president on a platform of economic reform and closer ties with Russia. Yet in 2003, he published a book called *Ukraine Is not Russia* (Kuchma, 2003). A skilful manager, Kuchma stabilized Ukraine both domestically and internationally and set it on a path of economic growth. However, the way in which he did this created a system of widespread corruption, which became difficult to root out. His political career ended in disgrace with the outbreak of the Orange Revolution in 2004.

When Kuchma took office, Ukraine was suffering from hyperinflation, internationally isolated and politically divided. Within a few years, Kuchma and his government stabilized the economy, introduced a national currency, embarked on a massive privatization programme, and diversified trade patterns. By 2000, the economy started growing and averaged 7.4 per cent real annual growth until 2007. Kuchma also signed the now infamous Budapest Memorandum in 1994 with the US, UK, and Russia, in which Ukraine gave up nuclear weapons in exchange for security guarantees from the other signatories. This improved international relations, and foreign aid finally began flowing into Ukraine. Negotiations with international institutions, including the EU and NATO, also advanced. In 1997, Russia finally agreed to sign a Friendship Treaty with Ukraine, which recognized the inviolability of both countries' borders, and that same year Russia signed the NATO–Russia Founding Act on Mutual Relations, Cooperation and Security.

Kuchma pushed through a new constitution in 1996, which among other things enshrined Ukrainian as the state language. The document was adopted in a dramatic overnight marathon parliamentary session. After years of preparation, political parties continued delaying and bickering, so Kuchma gave them a firm deadline. He threatened to dissolve parliament unless they agreed to a new constitution by 28 June, which they did. However, the continued political divisions made it difficult for Kuchma to govern, particularly as the Communist Party and others from the old guard still held power in parliament and opposed reforms. And the democrats had fragmented.

So Kuchma turned to the emerging business class. These were largely gangster capitalists who had accumulated tremendous wealth in dubious ways. But they were making change happen, and Kuchma used them as a vehicle for privatization and marketization. As one insider told the author at the time, the way it worked was people with money and the right contacts would come to Kuchma and say, 'This state business is failing; let me have it and I'll make it successful.' That is how a shady businessman, a filmmaker, and an American heir got the broadcast licence for one of the state television channels and turned it into the successful Studio 1+1, which grew into one of the two largest private media corporations in the country.

Oleksandr Tkachenko, who in 2020 became Ukraine's Minister of Culture and Information Policy, was the channel's first news editor and was given a free hand. He hired the best journalists in the country in what he described as a dream team that happens once in a lifetime. Media and information had been tightly controlled by Moscow during the communist era. After independence, Ukraine immediately took over broadcast signals on its territory, but there were only a handful of journalists who were independently minded. Tkachenko was one of them. He had pushed the envelope as far as he could while working on state-owned TV, and in 1991, after meeting with foreign journalist Susan Viets, he was hired to work for Reuters, becoming one of the first Ukrainians to work for a foreign media outlet. There, he learned about Western media standards. As soon as he was able to raise enough money, he launched his own small media company, NovaMova (New Talk). With the skills he had picked up at Reuters, Tkachenko created a new format for television news in Ukraine. When 1+1 was hiring, Tkachenko was a natural choice. Along with others recruited by the station, he had a cosmopolitan worldview and was determined to create a new kind of TV channel that was young, hip, and Ukrainian speaking. Another private company established at the same time, INTER, had a very different vision. Its team broadcast in Russian, sourced news from Moscow rather than producing its own, and showed lots of old Soviet-era films. Both channels attracted large audiences, which reflected how identity remained diverse in early post-Soviet Ukraine. Some people felt Ukrainian and cosmopolitan, while others had a residual Soviet or Russian mindset. These two divergent groups co-existed in the new state (Dyczok, 2009).

Within a year, Tkachenko was fired. He had been told he would have editorial freedom, but it soon became apparent that the president and his allies did not like being criticized on television, and warnings were sent to the station owners to soften their coverage. When Tkachenko insisted on reporting news objectively, he was told his services were no longer required. The same thing happened to his replacement Andriy Kulykov. The company's owners were vulnerable to political pressure: because of the non-transparent way in which they received their broadcast licence, it could just as easily be revoked.

Freedom of speech had been enshrined in Article 34 of Ukraine's new constitution, but Kuchma and most lawmakers still wanted to control the flow of information and viewed media as an instrument of power. Most state-owned media had been privatized, but some media outlets were kept in state hands for this reason, and Kuchma did not shy away from pressuring privately owned media when it suited his interests. By 1999, he was named one of the world's top enemies of free speech (CPJ, 2000).

The Oligarchs, Europeanists, and Revolutionaries

A key figure in Kuchma's economic success was the tall, handsome banker and economist Victor Yushchenko. Although best known internationally for being poisoned when running for president against Kuchma's candidate Victor Yanukovych in 2004, Yushchenko was once Kuchma's ally. Back in 1993, the son of teachers from the Sumy oblast near the Russian border was appointed the governor of the National Bank of Ukraine. Working in the historic 1905 building with its own rose garden and bakery, Yushchenko brought inflation down from more than 10,000 per cent to less than 10 per cent in just a few years. In 1996, he oversaw the introduction of Ukraine's new currency and managed to defend its value following the 1998 Russian financial crisis. Ukraine called its new currency the *hryvnia*. Although a bit hard to pronounce for foreigners, the name was deliberately chosen since it was used in the Kyivan Rus era. In 1999, Kuchma appointed Yushchenko as his prime minister, and the following year Ukraine's economy grew for the first time since independence.

Kuchma had stabilized Ukraine, but in the process he created a system that many call an oligarchy, which slowed down political reform and democratization. The non-transparent privatization process led to the emergence of a small group of extremely wealthy and powerful men called oligarchs who in effect owned and ran the country. Kuchma's son-in-law, Victor Pinchuk, was one of them. Political and economic elites became intertwined and interdependent. But Kuchma had divided state assets in such a way that no one person or group dominated, so there was built-in competition among the oligarchic clans. This prevented a single person or group from dominating the market and created some room for opposition. Not all the oligarchs were the same. They all enjoyed the privileges of wealth, vacationing in the Riviera, buying property abroad, and sending their children to the world's top universities. But while some looked towards the West, others continued to hold close ties with Russia. Pinchuk was one of the former. He created a contemporary art centre in Kyiv, naming it after himself, and began hosting Ukraine events at the annual Davos Summit in Switzerland. He also created the Yalta European Strategy, an annual forum held in Crimea's historic Livadia Palace, where European leaders were wined and dined while debating the future of Ukraine and the EU. Other oligarchs chose to maintain close ties with Russia, such as Victor Medvedchuk who became a godfather to Putin's youngest daughter Darya. Then there were oligarchs who tried to balance between the two, profiting from links with Russia while purchasing property in the West. But they all faced the same dilemma of wanting to be accepted in the world while playing by old rules.

On 13 September 2000, Kuchma travelled to Paris for the Ukraine–EU Summit and was welcomed as a successful reformer. Shortly after, he returned to Kyiv to face a scandal from which he would never recover. Opposition journalist Heorhii Gongadze from the online paper *Ukrainska Pravda* had disappeared, and not long after a headless corpse was discovered in the woods near Kyiv. Kuchma's adversary, Socialist Party leader Oleksandr Moroz, released audio tapes in which what sounds like Kuchma's voice says, among other things, 'Give me this one, about "Ukrainska Pravda" . . . (indecipherable). We will start to decide what to do with him. He has simply gone too far already . . . . I'm telling you, drive him out, throw him out. Give him to the Chechens. (Indecipherable) . . . and then a ransom' (Maksymiuk, 2005). It became known as 'Kuchmagate', and world leaders started to shun the Ukrainian president. At one international gathering name plates were written in French, the United States as États-Unis and the United Kingdom as Royaume-Uni, so their delegates would not have to sit next to Ukraine. The only country that continued to welcome Kuchma was Russia, now governed by a new president, Vladimir Putin.

When Kuchma's second presidential term was coming to an end, he tried to follow the Russian model of appointing his successor, which had worked for Yeltsin. He chose his new prime minister, Victor Yanukovych, a large oafish thug with an alleged criminal record who was an influential figure in the Donetsk clan, to run against his former star Yushchenko, who had been chosen to lead an electoral alliance called Our Ukraine and now had a new beautiful blonde American wife. It was a dirty campaign that included poisoning Yushchenko and election rigging. But as Kuchma himself had written, Ukraine is not Russia. Ukrainians had learned about exit polls, and when official results didn't match the polls, people took to the streets in what became known as the Orange Revolution. Maria Burmaka, now an established musician, joined others on an improvised stage in central Kyiv to call for a repeat vote.

After weeks of protests in the cold, a compromise was reached. New elections were held and Yushchenko won with a slim majority, 52 per cent. Russia immediately labelled the new Ukrainian president a CIA plant, citing his US wife as evidence, and called the Orange Revolution a 'Western plot'. It also announced it was more than tripling the price of its natural gas, which Ukraine was dependent on. After months of disputes over prices, in January 2006 Russia cut off gas supplies to Ukraine altogether. Ukraine responded by siphoning gas from the pipeline running through its territory that transported energy to European countries. They intervened, and after negotiations, the gas was turned on again. Russia then began making plans for an alternative gas pipeline to Europe called Nordstream that would bypass Ukraine.

Yushchenko was the first Ukrainian president to launch projects aimed at fostering a common identity to unite the country. During the first decade of independence, politicians were focused on survival, and society had been left to develop on its own. A vibrant civil society had begun to form, a new curriculum was introduced in schools and universities, but divisions persisted around issues of language, culture, history, and worldviews. In an effort to forge a unified national identity, Yushchenko spearheaded several important initiatives. He created an Institute of National Memory and appointed the young historian Volodymyr Viatrovych to head the former KGB archives and open up the documents from the past. He also repurposed a large factory, Arsenal, into a modern art centre and built a National Museum of the Holodomor-Genocide to commemorate Stalin's victims in the 1932–3 famine. He often wore traditional Ukrainian embroidered shirts with his jeans and organized meetings between veterans of the Red Army and the Ukrainian Insurgent Army (UPA), who had fought against each other in World War II, to help bring about reconciliation and heal old wounds.

At the international level, Yushchenko pursued closer ties with the European Union and NATO while maintaining relations with Russia. But at the political level, his presidency was less than effective. Opposition to Kuchma had united disparate political groups, but once Yushchenko was elected, that unity disappeared. Yulia Tymoshenko, known for her signature golden braid, was appointed prime minister, but she was soon at loggerheads with the president, so he dismissed her as well as other former allies. In what many considered a controversial move, in 2006, he chose his former foe Yanukovych for the prime minister's job and tried to dissolve parliament. A couple of years on, the 2008 global financial crisis hit Ukraine very hard, and Yushchenko's popularity dipped further. When he ran for re-election in 2010, he got the worst result of any sitting president in Ukraine's short history – 5.45 per cent. Yanukovych, who had undergone an image transformation with the help of US spin doctor Paul Manafort, won 48.95 per cent of the vote, narrowly beating Tymoshenko who received 45.7 per cent. She contested the results but with no success.

Yanukovych's presidency was probably the most corrupt era in Ukraine's modern history. He allowed his friends and allies, known as 'The Family', to raid businesses and the economy. stifled civil society, muzzled the media, and imprisoned political opponents. His rival Yulia Tymoshenko was accused of abusing power and embezzlement in a 2009 gas supply agreement with Russia and sent to jail for seven years after being forced to pay a $188-million fine. Meanwhile, Yanukovych, who came from humble beginnings, was living a lavish lifestyle. He built himself an opulent 140-hectare estate on former state land in Mezhyhiria just north of Kyiv. Behind a 16-foot fence and prison-like security there were artificial lakes, a spa, gym, tennis court, helipad, private petting zoo, and state-of-the-art lab for testing food. The interior of the house, with its garish décor, was found to be filled with farcical treasures that included a solid gold loaf of bread.

Yet while speaking mainly Russian and making concessions to Russia in Crimea, Yanukovych kept an open mind towards Europe. In 2012, Ukraine co-hosted the Euro Cup football match with Poland, which brought a record number of tourists and revenue to the country. Most importantly, Yanukovych continued negotiations with the EU on an Association Agreement. But things didn't go as planned. After years of rampant corruption, Ukraine's state coffers were almost empty, so Yanukovych embarked on a global tour seeking loans. When everyone else said no, he travelled to Moscow. This was a week before the third Eastern Partnership summit in Vilnius on 28–29 November 2013, where the much-anticipated EU–Ukraine Association Agreement was to be signed. While in Moscow, Yanukovych received a $15-billion aid package and instructed his prime minister to announce that the EU agreement was on hold. This enraged Ukrainians and they once again took to the streets in what is known as the Euromaidan protests, or the Revolution of Dignity.

Ukrainian society had changed in the decades since independence. Barriers to the outside world disappeared with the end of communism, and Ukrainians were able to travel, study, and live abroad. A middle class had emerged thanks to the economic reforms that arrived with marketization. An entire generation had grown up educated in a new, non-Soviet way, learning Ukrainian history from a non-Russian perspective. And large numbers of people were willing to stand up for their European choice.

Yanukovych failed to budge on his decision and sent riot police to disperse the protestors. This had the opposite effect: the protests grew, and they became more about the president's corrupt rule. Musicians entertained the demonstrators standing in snow-covered city squares, and once again Maria Burmaka was there singing her protest songs. Things came to a head on 18–20 February 2014 when, after months in the cold, protestors called for Yanukovych to be ousted and marched towards the parliament. Riot police started shooting at them, killing many. Yanukovych hopped on his private helicopter and eventually fled to Russia, but not before dumping tons of documents in his private lake, including evidence of his payments to US spin doctor Paul Manafort. Activists later fished them out, and the papers would come to haunt many people, including Manafort who in 2016 was running Donald Trump's presidential campaign.

The ousting of Yanukovych was a bittersweet victory for Ukrainians. They had overthrown a corrupt and unpopular president, but over 100 demonstrators had been killed in the process. These martyrs became known as the Heavenly Hundred. Yet as Ukrainians both celebrated their victory and buried their dead, few could have imagined what would come next. Within days they would go from defending their democracy and European choice to defending their state and their lives when Russia launched a stealth war against them in 2014 that escalated to a full invasion in 2022.

5 The Defenders

Introduction

'Russian warship go f*** yourself' became a global meme in 2022. That's what Ukrainian border guards told the *Moskva* cruiser on 24 February 2022 when they were ordered to surrender or be killed. Russia's Black Sea Fleet flagship threatened to bomb Ukraine's strategic Snake Island but the heavily outnumbered border guards refused to submit. This phrase captured the essence of Ukrainians' reaction to Russia's attack. Ukraine had made it clear that it considered itself part of Europe, and Russia responded in the old imperial way – with war. Russia probably didn't imagine that Ukrainians could or would resist. It also did not understand that although many Ukrainians spoke Russian and were sympathetic towards their country, they considered themselves a separate nation. They were Ukrainians, not Russians, and would fight to defend their independence. When Russian tanks advanced on the capital Kyiv, the US offered to evacuate Ukrainian president Volodymyr Zelensky, a Russian-speaking Jew from central Ukraine. He replied, 'The fight is here; I need ammunition, not a ride' (Braithwaite, 2022).

Through their actions in 2022 Ukrainians became the focus of the world's attention and once again affected the course of international relations. But the war had started eight years earlier. Phase one began in 2014. Russia launched a stealth annexation of Crimea and started war in Ukraine's eastern Donbas region while denying it was involved. This was followed by a long second phase, a simmering war that lasted from 2015 to 2022 with little headway by either side. Phase three started in February 2022. Russia escalated and launched a full-scale invasion which it called a 'special military operation to de-nazify Ukraine'.

Maria Berlinska was working on her master's degree in Jewish history in Kyiv and playing guitar in her spare time when Russia first invaded in 2014. The dark-haired student had actively participated in the Revolution of Dignity in the city's central square. When fighting broke out in the country's eastern Donbas region, she found a volunteer battalion that would take a woman with no military experience, signed up, and learned to operate aerial reconnaissance drones. She went on to champion women's rights in the army.

This was a new kind of war, a twenty-first-century war happening in the era of social media and global uncertainty. The world could watch on their screens as Russia killed Ukrainians and destroyed their cities while its propaganda machine distorted facts and claimed it was not at war with Ukraine. Fake news became part of international politics, and social media a double-edged sword. On the one hand, events were documented in photographs and videos, spreading globally in seconds. On the other hand, Russian troll factories circulated fake news with equal speed. Russia used disinformation not only against Ukraine but against all democratic countries, including the US.

How did the world respond? No country wanted to get involved in a military confrontation with a nuclear power. Yet international law had clearly been violated, and the war could spread, so something had to be done. But institutions like the United Nations, designed to maintain global peace, did not have any mechanisms to stop the war. They were barely coping with issues like climate change, extreme weather disasters, growing energy insecurity, a pandemic, humanitarian and migration crises, food insecurity, wars, cyberattacks, and the rise of fake news. Russia's war on Ukraine intensified these problems and caused new ones. At the time of writing, March 2024, the war was ongoing and had become the largest war in Europe since World War II. 'Never again' was happening again and this time the world was watching on their screens in real time.

The Volunteers

Russia first attacked Ukraine in late February 2014. The goal was to bring Ukraine back under Russian control by dismembering the country from the inside and turning it into a failed state while wrapping things in a disinformation fog. Covert measures like economic blackmail and cyber and psychological warfare had failed, so Russia escalated to the use of force. To a large degree, it was volunteers, ordinary Ukrainians like Maria Berlinska, who foiled Putin's plans. At that moment the Ukrainian state was very weak. The country had just experienced a revolution that had ended in bloodshed and with its president fleeing the country, so it was without a political leader. As Ukraine's parliament called an emergency session to appoint an interim president and prime minister and organize new elections, Russia sent unmarked troops into Crimea and secret operatives into eastern Ukraine.

The annexation of Crimea went smoothly. After the 2014 revolution Ukraine had set up an interim government but Russia began constructing a false story that a Western-financed 'fascist coup' had taken place in Kyiv and that the new government was persecuting Russians and Russian speakers. It called people to take to the streets. Some in Ukraine believed the story and organized anti-Kyiv rallies. On 27 February, Russian troops with no identifying insignia began taking over strategic sites on the Crimean Peninsula – Ukrainian military bases and ships, the airport, the communications systems, and the regional parliament. Ukrainians jokingly called them 'little green men' who had come from outer space because they refused to say who they were or where they had come from. These 'little green men' forcibly ousted the elected local government, replaced it with their puppet regime, and organized an event they called a 'referendum'. On 16 March, they announced that 96 per cent of Crimeans had voted to join Russia. Putin said they were reuniting with their 'historic homeland'. His domestic approval ratings shot up to 89 per cent, and that popular support would give him a free hand in Russia for the next few years.

Many countries condemned Russia's annexation of Crimea. Some imposed sanctions against Russia for violating Ukraine's territorial integrity and the United Nations passed a non-binding resolution (68/262) calling the Crimean referendum invalid. But all this had no impact.

Part of Putin's success in Crimea was because Russia constructed an effective historical propaganda campaign that 'Crimea has always been Russia.' Most of the world did not know Crimea's real history, that the Russian Empire had colonized the peninsula in the late eighteenth century and systematically displaced its Indigenous Crimean Tatar population. So some were prepared to believe the Kremlin's storyline. Russians too bought into the historical myth, since that is what they had always been taught.

Crimea was an easy target. Russia had its Black Sea Fleet harboured on the peninsula through a long-standing agreement with Ukraine, and it launched its troops from there. Pro-Russian sentiment had been high in Crimea since 1944, mainly because 58.5 per cent of its population were ethnic Russians, many of whom settled there after the Crimean Tatars had been deported under Stalin. Only 24.4 per cent were Ukrainians and 12.1 per cent Crimean Tatars. But pro-Russian sentiment and separatism are different things. In the last free election in Crimea in 2010, the separatist Russian Unity Party won only 4 per cent of the vote. When Russia invaded, it dissolved the democratically elected government and installed the Russian Unity Party leader Sergey Aksyonov as the new chief of Crimea. There were demonstrations against the 'little green men', and Crimean Tatars came out with their flags in peaceful rallies, but they were no match for the heavily armed Russian soldiers. Ukraine's armed forces did not intervene during this takeover, largely due to the power vacuum in the capital and its Western partners urging Kyiv not to take 'precipitate action'. Crimea's political and economic elites either accommodated the Russian takeover or left. Anyone who opposed Russia's actions was persecuted, imprisoned, and often tortured. Crimean Tatar leaders were put on a 'wanted list', and many people fled to other parts of Ukraine.

Russia's next target was southern and eastern Ukraine. But there, things did not go smoothly. Although there had always been a degree of pro-Russian sentiment in the region, there was no separatist violence until the spring of 2014. The pro-Russian protests that began in March 2014 had local support but were not spontaneous; rather, they were part of 'a carefully orchestrated campaign with Russian support' (Psaki, 2014). These protests were met with large pro-Ukrainian gatherings. Titushky, or paid provocateurs, often with criminal pasts, deliberately clashed with the pro-Ukrainian demonstrators, trying to intimidate them. The police did not always intervene. Protests occurred in eleven cities, but the worst confrontations happened in Donetsk and Luhansk, provinces that border Russia. Pro-Russian demonstrators began storming government offices and raising Russian flags. At times, the violence escalated to killing. Russian media portrayed these actions as a grassroots movement of 'pro-Russian separatists'. As the events were unfolding, it was hard to get a clear understanding of what was happening because the pro-Russian forces attacked journalists to stop them from reporting (Dyczok, 2015).

What later became clear was that many 'separatist' leaders were in fact Russian operatives, and Russia had provided armaments and funds to them and their supporters. One infamous character was the moustache-sporting Igor Girkin, also known by his alias Strelkov, which means shooter. Girkin was a Russian Army veteran and former secret service officer who received a gold medal from Putin for his role in annexing Crimea. He then went to Donetsk where he organized militant groups to fight against Ukraine, eventually becoming the leader of the separatist forces. The anti-Ukrainian militant groups succeeded in taking over parts of Luhansk and Donetsk, and in April they followed the Crimean pattern. They organized events they called 'referendums' and declared themselves the Luhansk and Donetsk 'People's Republics'. At this time, Putin began talking about a new 'Novorossiya (New Russia) Project', alluding to Catherine the Great's eighteenth-century imperial expansion and essentially weaponizing history. He wanted to create a land bridge to Crimea, extending it to the breakaway Transdniestria region in Moldova, which neighbours Ukraine on its south-western border.

But the anti-Ukrainian violence was stalled by ordinary Ukrainians who self-organized and pushed back. Semen Semenchenko was a short, stocky, Russian-speaking Ukrainian from Donetsk who studied to be a filmmaker. In the spring of 2014, when so-called separatists began taking over nearby towns and villages, he gathered some friends, formed a citizen militia, and confronted them. He wore a balaclava since Russia was using powerful face recognition software; he did not want to put his family at risk. This group would grow into the Donbas Battalion and eventually become part of Ukraine's official defence through the Interior Ministry and National Guard. It was one of many such groups that sprang up in the Donbas. These volunteer military battalions played a key role in stopping the war from escalating in 2014, but they have been subject to controversy because some held right-wing ideologies or accepted funding from oligarchs.

As Semen and people like him were taking up weapons to defend their towns and cities, others stepped up to help in different ways. Volunteer groups began collecting money and buying food, medical supplies, and equipment needed by the fighters, like the drones Maria Berlinska was learning to operate. Journalists and media professionals joined on the information front. Some went into the emerging war zone to try to report on what was happening on the ground since disinformation was widely being used as a weapon by Russia to cloud the issues. They were often attacked by anti-Ukrainian forces who did not want the world to see what they were doing. For journalists in Ukraine, 2014 became an especially dangerous year. Seven were killed, seventy-eight were kidnapped, and numerous others tortured. To get Ukraine's story out to the world, a group of public relations experts in Kyiv rented a hotel suite and set up a Ukraine Crisis Media Center. This created a space for press conferences where journalists could obtain information from government officials and civic activists.

Kyiv journalism professor Yevhen Fedchenko teamed up with some students and launched a novel initiative they called StopFake. They tracked the fake news coming from the Kremlin and then exposed it in their broadcasts.

One might be wondering why was all this coming from society – where was the state? In the spring of 2014, when Russia first attacked, the Ukrainian state was weak and ineffective. Years of corruption and a Russian fifth column had left the country in terrible shape. Its last defence minister, Pavlo Lebedyev, and the head of its security service, Oleksandr Yakymenko, both turned out to be Russian citizens and fled to Russia along with the president. Army units were sent to fight in the east and while achieving some successes, there were problems. The army had been cannibalized from the inside and its command structure was dysfunctional and unreliable. The same could be said of the National Guard, as well as the police, border, and security services. The state coffers were virtually empty, and government press services were in such poor shape that Ukraine was not getting its story out to the world. Russia was attacking militarily and succeeding in the information war.

The Presidents

Things changed when Petro Poroshenko was elected president on 25 May 2014, three months after his predecessor Yanukovych had decamped to Russia. The tall, square-faced billionaire was popularly known as the 'Chocolate King'. He had made a fortune in the confectionary business building the successful Roshen brand, which is sold internationally. But Poroshenko was also an experienced politician who had the know-how and clout to steer his country through what was then its worst crisis since independence. His challenge was how to stop the war and clean up corruption at the same time. Under his leadership, Ukraine fought Russia to a draw on the military front, blew holes in its propaganda campaign, increased cooperation with the European Union, and made substantial strides in reforming the state and its army.

Almost immediately after taking office, Poroshenko engaged in international negotiations to seek an end to the war and improve the country's economy. Even before his inauguration he was in touch with foreign leaders and created the Normandy Contact Group with France and Germany on the seventieth anniversary of D-Day, the symbolic beginning of the end of World War II. He also initiated diplomatic talks with Russia and brought the Organization for Security and Co-operation in Europe (OSCE) into what would become the Trilateral Contact Group on Ukraine. Poroshenko then travelled to the war zone and on 20 June 2014 declared a unilateral ten-day ceasefire to give the 'separatists' in the east a chance to withdraw.

But the Russian proxies were not interested in peace. They were pursuing Putin's 'Novorossiya' project and violated the ceasefire within days. The war escalated. Russia continued its propaganda that there was a 'civil war' in Ukraine and continued sending in heavy armaments. The world started to realize what was really happening in July of that year, when a Malaysian civilian airliner was shot down over Donetsk killing all 298 people onboard. At first, the downing of Flight MH17 was blamed on Ukraine, but it soon became clear that the BUK missile that took down the plane was from Russia. An international investigation was launched, and eight years later a Dutch court would find three men guilty of murder. One of them was the Russian operative Igor Girkin.

The summer and autumn of 2014 was a period of heavy fighting in the Donbas. Both sides tried to capture and keep territory. A particularly bloody confrontation happened in August in the town of Ilovaisk, where Ukrainian forces were surrounded. They negotiated a safe-passage evacuation corridor and then were slaughtered as they retreated. This led to renewed international concern, and the Trilateral Contact Group negotiated a peace plan called the Minsk Protocol. It was signed on 5 September 2014 by Ukraine, Russia, the OSCE, and the then-leaders of the self-proclaimed 'People's Republics' of Donetsk and Luhansk. This too failed to bring peace. Not long after, pro-Russian forces attacked the Donetsk International Airport and the drawn-out battle that followed became legendary. Ukrainian forces defended the airport so ferociously that Russians began calling them 'Cyborgs', implying that no humans could fight like that. Ukrainians embraced the nickname and soon songs were being composed about the valiant airport defenders. Ultimately though, the Ukrainians were forced to retreat from the destroyed airport and a new Minsk II Agreement was signed on 12 February 2015. Fighting subsided, at least for a time. France and Germany insisted that the document was the basis for seeking peace, but the agreement was never fully implemented and low-level fighting continued.

War became the new normal for Ukraine. It had lost 7 per cent of its territory – an important stretch of land that accounted for 20 per cent of its industrial output. Over two million people had fled from what became known as the Temporarily Occupied Territories and became internally displaced people, or IDPs. But for most Ukrainians, the war was far away, and it began to recede in their minds as they focused their attention on reforming their country.

A month into his presidency, Poroshenko signed the European Union–Ukraine Association Agreement, the same agreement that people had taken to the streets to fight for back in 2013. This brought Ukraine closer to its goal of reintegrating into Europe. Ukrainians could now freely travel to the EU, and trade became easier. By 2021, the EU had become Ukraine's largest trading partner, while trade with Russia dropped. Before the agreement, 25.7 per cent of Ukrainian exports went to Russia and 24.9 per cent to the EU. Six years later, exports to Russia fell to 7.7 per cent and the EU's share shot up to 42.6 per cent (Zachmann et al., 2020). The agreement also required Ukraine to transform its legislation to bring it to EU standards. This was a very important push to get

Ukraine moving on much-needed reforms in areas such as rules and procedures, standards, competition, protection of intellectual property rights, transparency, and best practices. Civil society was also advocating for reforms, especially those that would eliminate corruption.

Many reforms were indeed introduced. A major decentralization project was launched by the new prime minister Volodymyr Groysman. Decision-making power was transferred from the centre to the regional and local authorities, and this radically changed the country's governing system. It proved invaluable when Russia later escalated its military aggression because local leaders could take quick decisions and did not have to wait for approval from the capital. A new police force, the National Police of Ukraine, was created, and educated young people were hired who had not previously served in the police. State media was transformed into a public broadcaster, finally ending the old Soviet practice of state ownership and control. De-communization laws were passed to further cut ties with the Soviet era. Foreign-born ministers with no connections to the old guard were brought into the government as part of the anti-corruption drive. The state's finances were put in the hands of US-born Natalie Jaresko, economics were trusted to Lithuania's Aivaras Abromavicius, and health care to a reformer from Georgia, Aleksandre Kvitashvili. Eight new laws on the judiciary were adopted, all approved by international partners as best practices.

Since the country was at war, military reforms became a priority. The old army had been underfunded, demoralized, and headed by a number of generals with secret Russian citizenship, a fifth column. The first challenge was to find a reliable defence minister. It took eight months and only the fifth attempt proved successful – Stepan Poltorak was officially appointed on 14 October 2014 and served for the remainder of Poroshenko's presidential term. The size of the military was increased from 184,000 to 250,000 with 900,000 reservists, and the budget more than doubled to over $6 billion, up from $2.7 billion. This represented more than 6 per cent of the country's GDP. Training was improved, including training exercises with NATO countries. Women's legal status was changed so they were recognized as combatants and not just support staff, largely due to efforts by Maria Berlinska and her colleagues. In a short time, remarkable progress was achieved, and Ukraine was able to stall the Russian advance in the east. Poroshenko liked to say, 'We've built a modern army.' But problems remained with a lack of civilian oversight and transparency of procurements; in other words, how money was spent.

Corruption remained the single biggest challenge that Ukraine was still grappling with. During the Poroshenko presidency a lot was accomplished in this area. A robust civil society sector emerged that monitored anti-corruption reform, and a hybrid electronic government e-procurement system called

Prozorro (which means transparent) was introduced, partnering with business, government, and civil society. But far more needed to be done. Most importantly, people's attitudes needed to change and that takes time. Anti-corruption institutions were set up and new legislation adopted to improve transparency, in part because of pressure from international donors and civil society. Ukraine improved its ranking in the Transparency International corruption index, but it remained in the bottom third of countries, ahead of Mexico but behind Egypt. The foreign-born ministers were soon replaced, and government officials learned how to get around the new electronic system of declaring their income, with many transferring formal ownership of their assets to their relatives and continuing to evade taxes.

Poroshenko was accused of not abiding by all the reforms he himself was introducing. Part of the problem was that he couldn't break corrupt networks in the judiciary and was trying to reform the system while he was part of it. And he never succeeded in eliminating the fifth column. Pro-Russian politicians and businessmen continued to be part of Ukraine's political and economic spheres. Poroshenko's successes were not enough to satisfy society, and when elections came in March 2019, he was soundly defeated by a charismatic political newcomer.

That newcomer was a forty-one-year-old actor-businessman, Volodymyr Zelensky (Onuch and Hale, 2022). Born into a Jewish family in the central Ukrainian city of Kryvyi Rih, Zelensky grew up speaking Russian and got a law degree from the Kryvyi Rih branch of a Kyiv university. But showbusiness was what he wanted. He became a performer and created a successful company called Kvartal 95 that sold entertainment programming throughout the post-Soviet space. In 2015, his company created a popular TV sitcom called *Servant of the People*, which featured Zelensky as an honest history teacher who was elected president and went on to clean up corruption. Then life imitated art. Zelensky ran for president and won 73 per cent of the vote in a dramatic landslide victory. His new party, also named Servant of the People, went on to sweep the parliamentary election and won a clear majority (254 seats). No political party in the country had done that since Ukraine gained independence from the USSR. Their closest rival was far behind, with forty-three seats: the pro-Russian Platform for Life and Peace party. That party would get suspended in 2022 when Russia escalated war.

The political novice started his new career with unprecedented power. Holding not only the presidency but also a majority in parliament, Zelensky seemed poised for success. He presented his political programme, and it was the same as Poroshenko's – peace and an end to corruption. With such high expectations, it is not surprising that Zelensky could not meet them. After an initial success securing the release of thirty-five prisoners from Russia in

September, he ran into the same problem as his predecessor. Russia was not interested in peace, and fighting corruption was much tougher than it appeared to the political newcomer.

Zelensky faced many difficulties, and they included corruption within his own party. He did not fare much better on the international scene, running into the same old stumbling block as Poroshenko, namely that nobody was prepared to push Russia into peace. Then in the autumn of 2019, the Ukrainian leader unwittingly found himself at the centre of a major scandal with US president Donald Trump, who had tried to blackmail him into providing compromising information against his rival Joe Biden. What Zelensky assumed was a confidential conversation got leaked to the international press and used in the Trump impeachment hearings for the world to see. In that conversation, Zelensky had criticized France and Germany for not doing enough to help Ukraine, which did not help matters.

Tensions began mounting even more in 2021. In July, Putin published a long essay in which he once again repeated the old colonial narrative that Ukrainians were not a nation, and that Ukrainians and Russians were historically one people. Russia began amassing troops along Ukraine's borders, and by December the number reached around 100,000. Russia stated it was conducting 'routine exercises', but the US repeatedly warned Ukraine that its northern neighbour was planning to invade.

The attack came in the early hours of 24 February 2022. Russia launched full-scale war from three directions: north, east, and south, by air, land, and sea. Tanks and other assault vehicles started pouring across Ukraine's borders. For the first time since World War II, missiles rained down on Ukrainian cities while the Russian naval fleet attacked from the Black Sea. Putin wrapped these actions in another lie, calling the invasion a 'special military operation to de-nazify' Ukraine, and claiming that Russia had no other option because NATO was moving its war machine to Russia's borders.

The Ukrainians

Ukrainians from all walks of life stood up to defend themselves in a way that amazed the world. Max, whom the reader met in the introduction, and many like him rushed to sign up for military service. Unarmed civilians confronted tank convoys, shouting 'Russians go home!' usually in Russian. People hurled Molotov cocktails at the invaders through their car windows while fleeing their homes. Border guards on the Black Sea's Snake Island told Russia's flagship warship *Moskva* to go f*** itself when they were told to surrender on the first day of the invasion. Many took to social media to document the invasion and show the world what was happening and that's how the 'Russian warship' phrase became a popular meme.

Russia was expecting to take over Ukraine's capital within days and the rest of the country within months. It reportedly had a detailed plan outlining how to occupy the entire country, take control of its resources, and eradicate its identity. Putin was planning to install a puppet government, much like he did in Crimea, and had kill lists drafted, intimidation techniques prepared, and collaborators identified. After the planned capture of Kyiv, military operations would continue, and occupied regions would hold 'referendums' to join Russia. Those who opposed these moves would be imprisoned and tortured. Children would be deported to Russia for 'adoption'. Nuclear power stations were to be connected to the Russian energy grid, agricultural production was to be shipped to Russia, and Russian teachers brought in to teach a new Russian curriculum (Zabrodskyi et al., 2022).

But things did not go according to plan. Even though some Ukrainians collaborated with the invading forces and others fled abroad, most resisted. Russia had overestimated its own military might, as well as Ukraine's weakness, and had planned for a short war. Instead, its troops failed to seize the capital Kyiv or any other major city except Kherson. They were, however, able to initially capture another 15 per cent of Ukraine's territory, roughly the size of the American Midwest. But Russian forces were not prepared for the resistance they encountered from Ukrainians and nor were they initially ready for a prolonged war. After a few weeks, they began withdrawing from territories they had captured in the north-east. They left behind destruction and evidence of their atrocities and war crimes: torture chambers, mass graves, reports of systematic rape. Bucha, a small town near Kyiv, became world famous because the Russians retreated so fast that they left evidence of their atrocities and war crimes for the world to see – corpses of Ukrainian civilians with hands tied behind their backs were lying throughout the streets.

Fighting continued in the country's southern and eastern provinces, and in the spring, the dramatic battle for Mariupol, a port city on the southern Sea of Azov, captured international headlines for weeks. Ukrainian forces, including the Azov Regiment that had liberated Mariupol back in 2014, were outnumbered and surrounded. As Russia shelled the once vibrant city to the ground, Ukrainian forces moved to a Soviet-era factory complex called Azovstal and used it as their base and shelter for civilians. They put up such a heroic defence that they became yet another potent symbol of Ukraine's resistance. One young fighter with the nom de guerre 'Orest' (Dmytro Kozatsky) photographed their hellish lives under siege, posting his pictures on Instagram and turning the fighters into international heroes. But surrounded on all sides, they had no chance of winning, and Ukraine's president eventually told them to end the battle, saying 'Ukraine needs Ukrainian heroes alive.'

After a relative lull in fighting over the summer, Ukraine launched its first offensive in September 2022. Moscow was busy illegally deporting Ukrainian children to Russia and organizing more fake 'referendums', but Ukrainian fighters began pushing back Russian forces and liberating territories. By November, Kherson, a city in the south known for its watermelons, was again flying the Ukrainian and EU flags. Retreating Russian troops left behind evidence of yet more war crimes, as well as booby traps, mines, and destroyed infrastructure. In typical imperial fashion, they had also stripped the Kherson Art Museum of valuable art and artefacts. Ukraine's military advanced slowly, with much of the fighting shifting to World War I-style trench warfare. But danger increased for all Ukrainians. Russia was unable to make much progress on the front line so increasingly turned to terrorizing the entire country. It weaponized winter, intensified bombing of civilian infrastructure, especially the energy grid, plunging Ukrainians into cold and darkness.

Ukrainians resisted because they knew, as their foreign minister Dmytro Kuleba tweeted back in March 2022, 'If Russia wins, there will be no Ukraine. If Ukraine wins, there will be a new Russia.' But like the Mariupol defenders showed, Ukrainians were outmanned and outgunned. They appealed to the world for help. Leading that appeal was President Zelensky. His personal charisma, communication skills, and TV experience proved invaluable for staying in touch with society, dispelling Russian propaganda and getting Ukraine's message out to the world. Every day, and sometimes a few times a day, he recorded video messages and shared them on social media. In the early days of the war, when rumours were flying that he had fled the country, Zelensky posted a selfie video of himself in front of Kyiv's landmark House with Chimaeras, saying: 'Good morning, Ukrainians. Currently there are a lot of rumours appearing on the internet. Like that I am asking our army to put down their arms and evacuate. I am here. We are not putting down arms. We will be defending our country.' Soon his messages were being quoted by international media far more than Putin's repetitive declarations of 'Nazis in Ukraine' or NATO causing the war (Dyczok and Chung, 2022). Zelensky made a point of emphasizing that Ukraine was defending not only its freedom, but democracy and its values.

Many governments and international organizations responded. Russia's invasion was widely condemned in statements, public protests, petitions, and by countless public figures who openly criticized the country. Democracies began imposing sanctions on Russia, increasing aid to Ukraine, and banning Russian propaganda media outlets. Numerous global firms left or stopped doing business with Russia, and international cultural and sporting events stopped inviting

Russians. However, countries that were traditionally anti-American, such as China, India, Iran, and Arab regions, were initially sympathetic to Russia and shared the Russian viewpoint that NATO and the US had caused the war. Even Pope Francis, who condemned Russia's brutality and offered to mediate, said that NATO was 'barking at Russia's door' (Roberts, 2022).

NATO was in fact bending over backwards not to get involved since the last thing it wanted was to be at war with Russia. In early 2022 few believed that Ukrainians would, or could, actually defend themselves from Russia's superior military machine, which is why the US offered to evacuate the Ukrainian president. But when Ukrainians refused to surrender and instead fought back, Western democracies gradually began supplying Ukraine with arms. At first, these were only defensive weapons, but slowly shipments increased to include artillery, ammunition, tanks, rocket launchers, and drones. These weapons made it possible for Ukraine to continue fighting and gradually start pushing Russia back. Although the US became the overall largest donor of military aid, sending an unprecedented $20 billion over the first ten months of the full-scale invasion, proportionally tiny Estonia contributed the most in relative terms, over 1 per cent of its GDP. It was also one of the loudest to raise the alarm and call on others to help Ukraine. Poland, Ukraine's western neighbour, also contributed significantly and accepted the largest number of refugees. It was the Eastern European countries that had in the past been colonized by the Russian Empire and the Soviet Union that fully understood the threat Russia's war posed to them and the world.

Russia's escalation against Ukraine dramatically raised global danger levels. By marching its army towards Kyiv, Russia brought war much closer to NATO's borders at a time when the Kremlin was ramping up its anti-NATO rhetoric – war could spread. Russia also created the very real possibility of nuclear disaster when it began taking over Ukraine's nuclear power stations and turning them into war zones, as well as threatening to use nuclear weapons against Ukraine and its allies. Global food insecurity grew after Russia occupied some of Ukraine's agricultural heartland and blocked its ports. Not only did it steal grain and destroy crops, but for months Russia prevented Ukraine, a major exporter of food and fertilizer, from getting the harvest it was able to collect to the world's most vulnerable regions. The war also caused Europe's largest migration crisis since World War II, since close to nine million Ukrainians fled from bombardment to neighbouring countries. And Europe's energy security was threatened when Russia began to weaponize its gas exports. The post-World War II, international rules-based order and the security architecture of Europe were both under threat.

The problem was that there were few mechanisms in place to stop Russia. The country had nuclear weapons, so no country or alliance was ready to engage with it militarily. Its permanent seat at the UN Security Council meant Russia could block that body from taking any effective action. Democratic countries continued to send military and humanitarian aid to Ukraine but refused to get directly involved. Some even called for Ukraine to sit down with Russia and negotiate. Ukraine replied that it wanted peace, and in November 2022 presented a ten-point peace plan based on international principles. The plan involved transferring nuclear power stations to the UN International Atomic Energy Agency, securing global food and energy security, the release of prisoners and return of deportees, reaffirmation of Ukraine's territorial integrity, withdrawal of Russian troops from Ukrainian territory, justice, environmental protection, prevention of escalation, and a document confirming the end of the war. Ukraine proposed a peace plan while Russia continued to wage war.

The second year of the war was difficult. Months passed without any major changes on the battlefield, and with both Russia and Ukraine suffering heavy casualties. Ukraine's much-anticipated summer counter-offensive in 2023 achieved little. The country waited for more armaments from its allies, while Russia created a multi-layered defence and mined much of the territory it had occupied. Ukraine's advance was slow. But Russia was also unable to push forward and in August one of its most successful commanders, Wagner mercenary leader Yevgeny Prigozhin, led a mutiny that got very close to Moscow. It failed and he reportedly died in a plane crash under mysterious circumstances. By the end of 2023, Russia had gained less than 2 per cent more of Ukrainian territory.

Meanwhile, Ukraine was making quiet strides in the tech sector. The thirty-something-year-old Mykhailo Fedorov was Deputy Prime Minister for Innovation, Digital Transformation, and more. He was using his millennial savvy to bring digital solutions to the battlefield and government. Two days after Russia invaded, he contacted Elon Musk on Twitter and asked for Starlink. This is how Ukraine got the crucial technology and later Tesla Powerwalls. Fedorov continued his global networking and ramping up drone production at home. The Ukrainian drones were successfully used to attack Russia and its navy. An under-reported story internationally was how Ukraine pushed Russia's Black Sea Fleet out of the north-western Black Sea without having a navy of its own – it was the drones. This allowed shipping to resume in the Black Sea, and Ukraine could once more export its agricultural products by sea. This had a dual benefit: Ukraine could get its products to market, and global food insecurity was reduced.

In the second half of 2023, international attention started shifting away from Ukraine. Partly, this was war fatigue. But it intensified in the autumn when Hamas launched a surprise attack against Israel and war erupted in another region of the world. There was growing hesitation about supplying Ukraine with additional weapons and aid, and more voices began echoing the Russian narrative of the need for peace talks and allowing Russia to keep the territories it had occupied by force. Things were starting to look grim. But on 14 December 2023, Ukraine received some good news: European Union leaders had decided to open accession negotiations. This meant that Ukraine was finally invited to begin the process of becoming a member of the European family.

Conclusion

On 2 January 2024, Max, whom the reader met in the introduction, was still somewhere on the front line in Ukraine. He posted a new photo of himself video-chatting with his now four-year-old son on Facebook. He titled it, 'Yesterday I was a phone parent while my wife was working'. It was clear from his social media posts that Max was tired of being at war. But as a historian, he understood that if Ukraine was defeated, his son would not have much of a future. Russia's 'three-day war to capture Kyiv' had dragged into two years and was continuing. Both sides had suffered serious casualties, but neither was prepared to accept defeat. Russian public opinion polls showed that most Russians wanted the war to end, but they also wanted to keep the Ukrainian territory they had already occupied. This was unacceptable for Ukrainians. They were not willing to leave any of their people or land under Russian control, and despite feeling fatigue they remained unrelenting. As the David and Goliath struggle continued, it felt as though the nineteenth-century poet Taras Shevchenko was inspiring twenty-first-century Ukrainians with another of his famous phrases, *Boritesia, poborete* – keep fighting, you are sure to win.

The world was surprised at how forcefully Ukrainians defended themselves when Russia launched its all-out invasion in 2022. This was because relatively little was known about Ukraine, its people, or its history. Most knew of Ukraine as 'the' Ukraine, which is the Russian imperial perspective that presents Ukraine as part of Russia, something Russian president Putin continued to repeat.

As this Element and other books have shown, Ukraine and Russia have distinct histories. They are intertwined in complicated ways, but Kyiv is much older than Moscow, and the lands surrounding the two cities developed under different influences. Yet in typical colonial fashion, the Russian Empire wrote its history to its advantage, presenting the history of the people it came to rule as its own. Kyiv is central to the origin story that the Russian Empire constructed – saying that the grand Kyivan Rus was the cradle of their civilization is much more attractive than beginning the real story in Moscow, which rose to power only centuries later as the tax collector of the Golden Horde.

Ukraine lives on the border of Europe and Asia, and over its 1,000-year history it has been at the centre of many global transformations. Another one began in 2014 and Ukraine once again finds itself at its centre. Back in the Middle Ages, when the Mongols destroyed Kyiv as a political capital, the United States, China, and Russia did not exist as states. In the twenty-first century, they are now major powers.

Russia's modern president Putin aimed to eradicate Ukraine as an independent state, yet he has accomplished the opposite. The war consolidated Ukrainian society and put it in the international spotlight like never before. In 2022, Ukraine became one of the most searched topics on the internet and was constantly in the international headlines. What used to be widely seen as part of Russia or 'the' Ukraine became identified as Ukraine, no longer from the old colonial perspective. Within Ukraine, support for democracy, and membership in the EU and NATO increased even further.

Modern communications played a key role in this. The internet and social media made it possible to report on the war in real time, and for Ukrainians to communicate directly with each other and the world. Their actions revealed very clearly that Ukrainians and Russians were separate peoples, making very different choices. Ukraine was looking forward to the future and strengthening its relationship with the rest of Europe and the democratic world based on common values. Russia was looking backward and trying to re-establish its former imperial power.

At the time of writing, March 2024, the outcome of Russia's war against Ukraine was difficult to predict. Like so many others, Max's little boy, who was given the historical name Volodymyr, had to flee a war when he was only two years old. Regardless of the war's outcome, when he grows up and goes to university, Volodymyr won't have to explain to his classmates that he is from Ukraine and not 'the' Ukraine.

Further Reading

General Histories of Ukraine

Hrushevsky, M. (1891–1934). *Історія України-Руси/Istoriia Ukraïny-Rusy*. (History of Ukraine-Rus'). English translation (1997–2021). 10 volumes in 12 books. Toronto: Canadian Institute of Ukrainian Studies Press.

Hrytsak, Y. (2024). *A Brief History of Ukraine: The Forging of a Nation*. New York: Public Affairs.

Magocsi, P. R. (2010). *A History of Ukraine: The Land and Its Peoples*. 2nd ed. Toronto: University of Toronto Press.

Magocsi, P. R. and G. J. Matthews. (1985). *Ukraine, a Historical Atlas*. Toronto: University of Toronto Press.

Plokhy, S. (2015). *The Gates of Europe: A History of Ukraine*. New York: Basic Books.

Rudnytsky, I. L. (1987). *Essays in Modern Ukrainian History*. Edmonton: Canadian Institute of Ukrainian Studies.

Subtelny, O. (2009). *Ukraine: A History*. 4th ed. Toronto: University of Toronto Press.

The Princes

Curta, F. (2019). *Eastern Europe in the Middle Ages (500–1300)*. Brill's Companions to European History, 2 vols. Leiden: Brill.

Duczko, W. (2004). *Viking Rus: Studies on the Presence of Scandinavians in Eastern Europe*. The Northern World. Leiden: Brill.

Franklin, S. and J. Shepard. (1996). *The Emergence of Rus, c. 950–1300*. Longman History of Russia. London: Longman.

Jackson, T. N. (2019). *Eastern Europe in Icelandic Sagas*. Leeds: ARC Humanities Press.

Mykhaylovskiy, V. (2019). *European Expansion and the Contested Borderlands of Late Medieval Podillya, Ukraine*. Leeds: ARC Humanities Press.

Plokhy, S. (2006). *The Origins of the Slavic Nations: Premodern Identities in Russia, Ukraine, and Belarus*. Cambridge: Cambridge University Press.

Raffensperger, C. (2012.) *Reimagining Europe: Kievan Rus' in the Medieval World*. Cambridge, MA: Harvard University Press.

Shepard, J. (2007). "Rus'" in Nora Berend (ed) *Christianization and the Rise of Christian Monarchy: Scandinavia, Central Europe and Rus' c. 900–1200*. . . . Cambridge: Cambridge University Press, 369–416.

Zajac, T. (2018). "The Social-Political Roles of the Princess in Kyivan Rus', ca. 945–1240" in E. Woodacre (ed.) *A Companion to Global Queenship...* Leeds: ARC Humanities Press/Amsterdam University Press, 125–146.

The Cossacks

Glaser, A., ed. (2015). *Stories of Khmelnytsky: Competing Literary Legacies of the 1648 Cossack Uprising*. Stanford, CA: Stanford University Press.

Gudziak, B. A. (1998). *Crisis and Reform: The Kyivan Metropolitanate, the Patriarch of Constantinople, and the Genesis of the Union of Brest*. Cambridge, MA: Harvard Ukrainian Research Institute – Harvard University Press.

Kohut, Z. E. (1988). *Russian Centralism and Ukrainian Autonomy: Imperial Absorption of the Hetmanate, 1760s–1830s*. Cambridge, MA: Harvard Ukrainian Research Institute – Harvard University Press.

Kohut, Z. E. (2024). *The Making of Cossack Ukraine: Political Thought, Culture, and Identity Formation, 1569–1714*. Montreal: Canadian Institute of Ukrainian Studies Press–McGill-Queens University Press.

Kohut, Z. E., V. Sklokin, and F. E. Sysyn, eds. (2023). *Eighteenth-Century Ukraine: New Perspectives on Social, Cultural, and Intellectual History*. Montreal: Canadian Institute of Ukrainian Studies Press–McGill-Queens University Press.

Plokhy, S. (2001). *The Cossacks and Religion in Early Modern Ukraine*. Oxford: Oxford University Press.

Plokhy, S. (2006). *The Origins of the Slavic Nations: Premodern Identities in Russia, Ukraine, and Belarus*. Cambridge: Cambridge University Press.

Ševčenko, I. (2009). *Ukraine between East and West: Essays on Cultural History to the Early Eighteenth Century*, 2nd ed. Toronto: Canadian Institute of Ukrainian Studies Press.

Sysyn, F. E. (1985). *Between Poland and the Ukraine: The Dilemma of Adam Kysil, 1600–1653*. Cambridge, MA: Harvard Ukrainian Research Institute – Harvard University Press.

Yakovleva, T. T. (2020). *Ivan Mazepa and the Russian Empire*. Montreal: Canadian Institute of Ukrainian Studies Press–McGill-Queens University Press.

The Nation Builders

Andriewsky, O. (2003). 'The Russian-Ukrainian Discourse and the Failure of the "Little-Russian Solution," 1782–1917' in A. Kappeler, Z. Kohut, F. Sysyn and M. von Hagen (eds.) *Culture, Nation, and Identity: The Ukrainian-Russian Encounter, 1600–1945*. Edmonton: Canadian Institute of Ukrainian Studies Press, 182–234.

Baumann, F. (2023). *Dynasty Divided: A Family History of Russian and Ukrainian Nationalism*. Ithaca, NY: Cornell University of Press.

Bilenkyi, S. (2023). *Laboratory of Modernity: Ukraine between Empire and Nation, 1772–1914*. Montreal: Canadian Institute of Ukrainian Studies Press.

Himka, J. P. (1999). 'The Construction of Nationality in Galician Rus': Icarian Flights in Almost All Directions', in R. G. Suny and M. D. Kennedy (eds.) *Intellectuals and the Articulation of the Nation*. Ann Arbor, MI: University of Michigan Press, 109–64.

Hunchak, T. and J. T. Von der Heide. (1977). *The Ukraine, 1917–1921: A Study in Revolution*. Cambridge, MA: Harvard Ukrainian Research Institute – Harvard University Press.

Klid, B. and A. J. Motyl. (2012). *The Holodomor Reader: A Sourcebook on the Famine of 1932–1933 in Ukraine*. Toronto: Canadian Institute of Ukrainian Studies Press.

Krawchenko, B. (1985). *Social Change and National Consciousness in Twentieth-Century Ukraine*. Houndmills: Macmillan in association with St Antony's College, Oxford.

Magocsi, P. R., (2002). *The Roots of Ukrainian Nationalism: Galicia as Ukraine's Piedmont*. Toronto: University of Toronto Press.

Plokhy, S. (2005). *Unmaking Imperial Russia: Mykhailo Hrushevsky and the Writing of Ukrainian History*. Toronto: University of Toronto Press.

Yekelchyk, S. (2007). *Ukraine: Birth of a Modern Nation*. Oxford: Oxford University Press.

Zayarnyuk, A. (2013). *Framing the Ukrainian Peasantry in Habsburg Galicia, 1846–1914*. Edmonton: Canadian Institute of Ukrainian Studies Press.

The State Builders

D'Anieri, P. J. (2023) *Ukraine and Russia: From Civilized Divorce to Uncivil War*. Cambridge: Cambridge University Press.

Dyczok, M. (2000). *Ukraine: Movement without Change, Change without Movement*. Amsterdam: Harwood Academic Publishers.

Harasymiw, B. (2002). *Post-Communist Ukraine*. Edmonton: Canadian Institute of Ukrainian Studies Press.

Karatnycky, A. (2024.) *Battleground Ukraine: From Independence to the War with Russia*. New Haven, CT: Yale University Press.

Kuzio, T. and A. Wilson. (1994) *Ukraine: Perestroika to Independence*. Basingstoke: Macmillan.

Marples, D. R. and F. V. Mills, eds. (2015). *Ukraine's Euromaidan: Analyses of a Civil Revolution*. Stuttgart: Ibidem-Verlag.

Minakov, M., H. V. Kas/iāñov, and M., Rojansky, eds. (2021). *From 'the Ukraine' to Ukraine: A Contemporary History, 1991–2021.* Stuttgart: ibidem-Verlag.

Pikulicka-Wilczewska, A. and R. Sakwa, eds. (2015). *Ukraine and Russia: People, Politics, Propaganda and Perspectives.* Bristol: E-International Relations. www.e-ir.info/publication/ukraine-and-russia-people-politics-propaganda-and-perspectives/.

Szporluk, R. (1997). 'Ukraine: From an Imperial Periphery to a Sovereign State'. *Daedalus*, 126(3): 85–119.

Szporluk, R. (2000). *Russia, Ukraine, and the Breakup of the Soviet Union.* Stanford, CA: Hoover Institution Press.

The Defenders

Aseev, S. (2023). *The Torture Camp on Paradise Street.* Z. Tompkins and N. Murray (translators). Cambridge, MA: Harvard University Press.

Edele, M. (2023). *Russia's War Against Ukraine. The Whole Story.* Melbourne: Melbourne University Press.

Finkel, E. (2024). *Intent to Destroy. Russia's Two-Hundred-Year Quest to Dominate Ukraine.* New York: Basic Books.

Harding, L. (2022). *Invasion: The Inside Story of Russia's Bloody War and Ukraine's Fight for Survival.* New York: Knopf Doubleday Publishing Group.

Onuch, O. and H. E. Hale. (2023). *The Zelensky Effect.* New York: Oxford University Press.

Plokhy, S. (2023). *The Russo-Ukrainian War: The Return of History.* London: Allen Lane.

Ponomarenko, Illia. (2024). *I Will Show You How It Was: The Story of Wartime Kyiv.* London: Bloomsbury Publishing.

Popova, M. and O. Shevel. (2024). *Russia and Ukraine: Entangled Histories, Diverging States.* Cambridge: Polity Press.

Sasse, G. (2023). *Russia's War Against Ukraine.* Cambridge: Polity Press.

Trofimov, Y. (2024). *Our Enemies Will Vanish: The Russian Invasion and Ukraine's War of Independence.* New York: Penguin Publishing Group.

References

Bilenky, S. (2012). *Romantic Nationalism in Eastern Europe: Russian, Polish, and Ukrainian Political Imaginations*. Stanford, CA: Stanford University Press.

Braithwaite, S. (2022). 'Zelensky Refuses US Offer to Evacuate, Saying "I Need Ammunition, not a Ride"'. *CNN News*, 26 February. www.cnn.com/2022/02/26/europe/ukraine-zelensky-evacuation-intl/index.html.

Brzezinski, Z. (1994). 'The Premature Partnership'. *Foreign Affairs*, 73(2): 67–82. https://doi.org/10.2307/20045920.

Carr, E. H. (1986). *What Is History?* 2nd ed. Basingstoke: Macmillan.

Committee to Protect Journalists (CPJ). (2000). 'Attacks on the Press 1999: Enemies of the Press'. 22 March. https://cpj.org/2000/03/title-74/.

Duczko, W. (2004). *Viking Rus: Studies on the Presence of Scandinavians in Eastern Europe*. The Northern World, 12. Leiden: Brill.

Dyczok, M. (2009). 'Ukraine's Changing Communicative Space: Destination Europe or the Soviet Past?' in L. M. L. Zaleska Onyshkevych and M. G. Rewakowicz (eds.) *Contemporary Ukraine and Its European Cultural Identity*. New York: M. E. Sharpe: 375–394.

Dyczok, M. (2015). 'The Ukraine Story in Western Media', in A. Pikulicka-Wilczewska and R. Sakwa (eds.) *Ukraine and Russia: People, Politics, Propaganda, and Perspectives*. London: e-international relations. www.e-ir.info/2015/04/30/the-ukraine-story-in-western-media/.

Dyczok, M. and Y. Chung. (2022). 'Zelens′kyi Uses His Communication Skills as a Weapon of War'. *Canadian Slavonic Papers/Revue Canadienne des Slavistes*, 64(2–3): 146–161. www.tandfonline.com/doi/full/10.1080/00085006.2022.2106699.

Edele, M. (2021). *Stalinism at War: The Soviet Union in World War II*. London: Bloomsbury Publishing.

Garnett, S. W. (1997). *Keystone in the Arch: Ukraine in the Emerging Security Environment of Central and Eastern Europe*. Washington, DC: Carnegie Endowment for International Peace.

Graber, K. (2022). 'It's Ukraine,' Not "the Ukraine" – Here's Why'. *The Conversation*, 9 March. https://theconversation.com/its-ukraine-not-the-ukraine-heres-why-178748.

Gromelski, T. (2013). 'Liberty and Liberties in Early Modern Poland–Lithuania', in S. Quentin and M. van Gelderen (eds.) *Freedom and the Construction of Europe*. New York: Cambridge University Press: 215–34.

Higasi, M. (2017). 'Watch as 1000 Years of European Borders Change (Time Lapse)'. Online video clip. www.youtube.com/watch?v=M90C7FA4FYU.

Hroch, M. (1996). 'From National Movement to the Fully-Formed Nation: The Nation-Building Process in Europe', in G. Eley and R. G. Suny (eds.) *Becoming National: A Reader*. New York: Oxford University Press, 59–77.

Hrushevsky, M. (1891–1934). *Історія України-Руси/Istoriia Ukraïny-Rusy* ('History of Ukraine-Rus'). English translation (1997–2021), 10 volumes in 12 books. Toronto: Canadian Institute of Ukrainian Studies Press.

Karamzin, N. (1816–29). *История государства Российского/Istoriia gosudarstva rossiiskogo* ('The History of the Russian State'), 12 vols. St Petersburg.

Kohut, Z. (1988). *Russian Centralism and Ukrainian Autonomy: Imperial Absorption of the Hetmanate, 1760s–1830s*. Cambridge, MA: Harvard University Press.

Konieczny, P. (2021). 'From Xenophobia to Golden Age: "Jewish Paradise" Proverb as a Linguistic Reclamation'. *Contemporary Jewry*, 41(2): 517–537. https://doi.org/10.1007/s12397-021-09380-4.

Kuchma, L. (2003). *Украина – не Россия. / Ukraina – ne Rosiia* ('Ukraine is not Russia'). Moscow: Vremya.

Kuleba, D. (@DmytroKuleba) (2022). 'If Russia wins, there will be no Ukraine; if Ukraine wins, there will be a new Russia'. Twitter, 25 March 2022, 7:21 PM, retweeted by Sabanadze, N. @natasabanadze. (2022). '"If Russia wins, there will be no Ukraine; if Ukraine wins, there will be a new Russia", said FM @DmytroKuleba So True. #SupportUkraine'. Twitter, 25 March 2022, 7:21 pm, https://twitter.com/natasabanadze/status/1507497928587415555.

Lieven, D. (2015). *The End of Tsarist Russia: The March to World War I and Revolution*. New York: Viking.

Lysenko, S. (2021). *Колапс: як українці зруйнували імперію зла* ('Collapse: How Ukrainians Destroyed the Evil Empire: Ukraine'). UA Pershy TV documentary series. www.youtube.com/@SuspilneNews/search?query=THE%20COLLAPSE%20How%20Ukrainians%20Destroyed%20The%20Evil%20Empire. Episode 6: Independence. www.youtube.com/watch?v=uudL79TOp7w&t=1454s; Episode 7: On the Verge of Nuclear War. www.youtube.com/watch?v=k6izGwSQwcs.

Mackinder, H. J. (1919). *Democratic Ideals and Reality: The Geographical Pivot of History*. New York: Henry Holt and Company Inc.

MacMillan, M. (2008). *The Uses and Abuses of History*. Toronto: Viking Canada.

Magocsi, P. R. (2010). *A History of Ukraine: The Land and Its Peoples*. 2nd ed. Toronto: University of Toronto Press.

Magocsi, P. R. and G. G. Matthews (Cartographer). (1987). *Ukraine: A Historical Atlas*. 2nd ed. Toronto: University of Toronto Press.

Maksymiuk, J. (2005). 'Transcript: What do Melnychenko's Tapes Say about Gongadze Case?' Radio Free Europe/Radio Liberty (RFE/RL), 3 March. www.rferl.org/a/1057789.html.

Martin, T. (2001). *The Affirmative Action Empire: Nations and Nationalism in the Soviet Union, 1923–1939*. Ithaca, NY: Cornell University Press.

Mayr, E. (2011). *Understanding Human Agency*. Oxford: Oxford University Press.

Onuch, O. and H. Hale. (2022). *The Zelensky Effect*. London: C Hurst & Company.

Plokhii, S. (2014). *The Last Empire: The Final Days of the Soviet Union*. New York: Basic Books.

Plokhii, S. (2016). *The Man with the Poison Gun: A Cold War Spy Story*. New York: Basic Books.

Psaki, J. (2014). 'US Department of State Daily Press Briefing'. Washington, DC. 7 April. https://2009-2017.state.gov/r/pa/prs/dpb/2014/04/224477.htm.

Putin, V. (2021). 'On the Historical Unity of Russians and Ukrainians'. President of Russia. Article. 12 July. http://en.kremlin.ru/events/president/news/66181.

Roberts, H. (2022). 'Pope Says NATO May Have Caused Russia's Invasion of Ukraine'. *Politico*, 3 May. www.politico.eu/article/pope-francis-nato-cause-ukraine-invasion-russia/.

Rudnytsky, I. L. (1987). *Essays in Modern Ukrainian History*. Edmonton: Canadian Institute of Ukrainian Studies.

Seegel, S. (2013). *Ukraine under Western Eyes*. Cambridge, MA: Harvard University Press.

Shuster, S. (2022). 'TIME 2022 Person of the Year: Volodymyr Zelensky'. *TIME Magazine*, 7 December. https://time.com/person-of-the-year-2022-volodymyr-zelensky/.

Snyder, T. (2022). The Making of Modern Ukraine. Class 12. Habsburg Curiosity. Yale Courses. www.youtube.com/watch?v=WO_SuY-4Sow.

StopFake. www.stopfake.org/en/main/.

Sviezhentsev, M. (2022a). '*Оце потрапив я повноцінно в фб*/finally have proper Facebook access'. Facebook, 14 June 2022, 2:31 am, www.facebook.com/max.svyezhentsev/posts/pfbid035SW5uYuuLAktkyqC8vsKBBgV9Mw3Y36gBneTxzxiMgeQRShCrhEccBTmvTgsmmZ8l; www.facebook.com/max.svyezhentsev/.

Sviezhentsev, M. (2022b). Screenshot by Volodymyr Sviezhentsev😀😎. Facebook, 22 June 2022, 8:17 am, www.facebook.com/max.svyezhentsev/posts/pfbid02c3iLs92dQtQS4BBGiCtHxvMK1SfvzCKNHbLpv8U6TnYD94y1Ph4WuwDZ1KMaKs78l; www.facebook.com/max.svyezhentsev/.

Sysyn, F. E. (2003). The Khmel'nyts'kyi Uprising: A Characterization of the Ukrainian Revolt. *Jewish History*, 17: 115–139.

Tolz, V. (2001). *Russia: Inventing the Nation*. London: Bloomsbury Publishing.

Ukraine Crisis Media Center. https://uacrisis.org/en/.

Yekelchyk, S. (2007). *Ukraine: Birth of a Modern Nation*. New York: Oxford University Press.

Zabrodskyi, M., J. Watling, O. V. Danylyuk, and N. Reynolds. (2022). *Preliminary Lessons in Conventional Warfighting from Russia's Invasion of Ukraine: February–July 2022*. Royal United Services Institute for Defence and Security Studies, Special Report. 30 November. https://rusi.org/explore-our-research/publications/special-resources/preliminary-lessons-conventional-warfighting-russias-invasion-ukraine-february-july-2022.

Zachmann, G., M. Dabrowski, and M. Dominguez-Jimenez. (2020). 'Ukraine: Trade Reorientation from Russia to the EU'. Bruegel blog post, 13 July. www.bruegel.org/blog-post/ukraine-trade-reorientation-russia-eu.

Zajac, T. (2018). 'The Social-Political Roles of the Princess in Kyivan Rus', ca. 945–1240' in E. Woodacre (ed.) *A Companion to Global Queenship*. Leeds: ARC Humanities Press/Amsterdam University Press: 125–146.

Zayarnyuk, A. (2022). 'Historians as Enablers? Historiography, Imperialism, and the Legitimization of Russian Aggression'. *East/West: Journal of Ukrainian Studies*, 9(2). https://doi.org/10.21226/ewjus754.

Zelenskyy, V. @ZelenskyyUa (2022). 'Ne virte feikam / Don't believe fakes'. Twitter, 26 February 2022, 12:57 am, https://twitter.com/ZelenskyyUa/status/1497450853380280320.

Acknowledgements

When Mark Edele invited me to submit a manuscript for this new series I immediately agreed. I had long wanted to write a volume explaining Ukraine to a general audience. Interest in Ukraine peaked following Russia's full-scale invasion in 2022 and it seemed the perfect time. Of course, I had no idea how hard it would be to put 1,000 years of history into 30,000 words in a way that was easy to understand and interesting to read for an informed but non-specialist audience. Fortunately, colleagues, friends, students, and former students helped by reading drafts of chapters, engaging in conversations, challenging my ideas, and giving excellent suggestions. Anonymous reviewers provided tremendously useful feedback, all of which I am extremely grateful for. Special thanks to Max Sviezhentsev, my former PhD student whom the reader met in the Element. He signed up to defend Ukraine in February 2022, and despite being on the front line he found time to read my work and provide feedback. I would like to thank my editors, the great Mark Edele and Rebecca Friedman, for all their patience and help. Also, sincere thanks to all these amazing people, in alphabetical order: Serhiy Bilenky, Yerin Chung, Steven Freedman, Paul Grajauskas, Roma Ihnatowycz, Andriy Kulykov, Ali Leon, Elizabeth Mantz, Barbara McGrath, Skip (Malcolm) McGrath, Khrystyna Nyshchei, Maria Popova, Tanya Richardson, Frank Sysyn, Susan Viets, Roman Waschuk, Alexander Wood-Balsom, Serhy Yekelchyk, and Talia Zajac. Any errors that remain in this Element are mine and mine alone.

Cambridge Elements

Soviet and Post-Soviet History

Mark Edele
University of Melbourne

Mark Edele teaches Soviet history at the University of Melbourne, where he is Hansen Professor in History and Deputy Dean in the Faculty of Arts. His most recent books are *Stalinism at War* (2021) and *Russia's War Against Ukraine* (2023). He is one of the convenors of the Research Initiative on Post-Soviet Space (RIPSS) at the University of Melbourne.

Rebecca Friedman
Florida International University

Rebecca Friedman is Founding Director of the Wolfsonian Public Humanities Lab and Professor of History at Florida International University in Miami. Her recent book, Modernity, Domesticity and Temporality: Time at Home, supported by the National Endowment for the Humanities, explores modern time and home in twentieth century Russia (2020). She is one of the editors for the Bloomsbury Academic series A Cultural History of Time.

About the Series

Elements in Soviet and Post-Soviet History pluralise the history of the former Soviet space. Contributions decolonise Soviet history and provincialise the former metropole: Russia. In doing so, the series provides an up-to-date history of the present of the region formerly known as the Soviet Union.

Cambridge Elements

Soviet and Post-Soviet History

Elements in the Series

Making National Diasporas: Soviet-Era Migrations and Post-Soviet Consequences
Lewis H. Siegelbaum and Leslie Page Moch

Ukraine not 'the' Ukraine
Marta Dyczok

A full series listing is available at: www.cambridge.org/ESPH

For EU product safety concerns, contact us at Calle de José Abascal, 56–1°,
28003 Madrid, Spain or eugpsr@cambridge.org.

www.ingramcontent.com/pod-product-compliance
Ingram Content Group UK Ltd.
Pitfield, Milton Keynes, MK11 3LW, UK
UKHW021326180426
11947UKWH00017B/1456